IMPROVING COMPUTER SCIENCE EDUCATION

IMPROVING

Computer Science

EDUCATION

Edited by

Djordje M. Kadijevich
Mathematical Institute, Serbian Academy of Sciences and Arts, Serbia

Charoula Angeli
Department of Education, University of Cyprus, Cyprus

Carsten Schulte
Department of Computer Science Education, Freie Universität Berlin, Germany

New York and London

First published 2013
by Routledge
711 Third Avenue, New York, NY 10017

Simultaneously published in the UK
by Routledge
2 Park Square, Milton Park, Abingdon, Oxon OX14 4RN

Routledge is an imprint of the Taylor & Francis Group, an informa business

Library of Congress Cataloging in Publication Data
Improving computer science education / edited by Djordje M. Kadijevich,
Charoula Angeli, and Carsten Schulte.
pages cm
Includes bibliographical references and index.
1. Computer science--Study and teaching. 2. Computer science--Study and teaching
(Secondary) I. Kadijevich, Djordje M. II. Angeli, Charoula. III. Schulte, Carsten.
QA76.27.I46 2013
004.07--dc23
2012033745

ISBN 978-0-415-64474-7 (hbk)
ISBN 978-0-415-64537-9 (pbk)
ISBN 978-0-203-07872-3 (ebk)

Typeset in Chaparral by the contributors
Book cover design and page layout by Djordje M. Kadijevich

Editor: Alex Masulis
Production editor: Alf Symons
Copy-editor: Tony Nixon

SUSTAINABLE
FORESTRY
INITIATIVE

Certified Sourcing
www.sfiprogram.org
SFI-00555
The SFI label applies to the text stock.

Printed and bound in the United States of America by
Walsworth Publishing Company, Marceline, MO.

CONTENTS

Part 3 Improving teaching

FOREWORD

Knowledge about computer science is a critical 21st Century literacy for citizens in the developed world. Students interact with computing every day of their lives. We accept that students ought to understand physical and natural sciences (e.g., chemistry, biology, and physics) in order to appreciate a scientific perspective and understand the world in which they live. In the same way, they ought to know something about the computer science that underlies the computational world in which they also live, including how the computational world was designed and created.

We have been teaching traditional sciences for far longer. We understand well the challenges of helping students develop scientific literacy. We know how to prepare teachers to teach science.

Computer science as a field is just over a half century old. We have only just started to teach computer science in schools. We know far too little about what challenges students will face and how to prepare teachers to teach computer science.

An interesting contrast is between the teacher professional organizations for mathematics and computer science. The *National Council for Teachers of Mathematics* (NCTM) in the United States was founded in 1920, so it's nearly 100 years old. The comparable *Computer Science Teachers Association* was just founded in 2005.

This book helps us in addressing the needs in preparing computer science teachers. Its editors have done an excellent job of gathering some of the best in the field to tell us what they know about the challenges of students learning computer science and about approaches for teaching computer science. We have a great deal of work to do in order to understand computer science education at the same depth as science education. This book helps us progress toward that goal.

Mark Guzdial
College of Computing
Georgia Institute of Technology

PREFACE

Traditionally, the teaching of school computer science has been focused on skills and decontextualized from real life. Currently, there is a strong research interest in situating the teaching of computer science education courses in rich learning activities that are authentic and relevant to students' lives.

In some European countries the term "computer science" is used to refer to the computer science curriculum students are taught in school, while in some other European countries the term "informatics" is preferred. The term "computing" is also used in some countries, but mostly in tertiary education contexts. The report *IFIP – UNESCO ICT 2006 Curriculum for Secondary Schools* uses the terms "informatics" and "computing science" as synonyms. In this book, we adopted the term "computer science" from the report *CSTA K-12 Computer Science Standards Revised 2011* to denote "the study of computers and algorithmic processes, including their principles, their hardware and software designs, their applications, and their impact on society" (p. 1).

The authors in this book describe their efforts toward approaching the teaching of computer science content in learner-centered ways, taking into consideration learners' difficulties in understanding the content, or teachers' difficulties in teaching or presenting the content adequately. The book consists of nine chapters divided equally into three sections. Each chapter in the book concludes with recommendations for teacher professional development; therefore, this book is suitable to be used as a textbook in graduate computer science education courses as well as by teacher educators in pre-service and in-service computer science or informatics courses.

The first part of the book, *Improving learning*, comprises a chapter on text comprehension, a chapter on spreadsheet learning, and a chapter on personalized database learning. The three chapters capitalize on the complexity of computer science learning and provide techniques about how to improve it.

The second part of the book, *Methodological perspectives*, consists of a chapter on the visualization of programming, a chapter on unplugging computer science, and a chapter on automatic and semi-automatic assessment of programming. These chapters deal primarily with methodological aspects of how to improve teaching and learning in computer science.

The third and last part of the book, *Improving teaching*, comprises a chapter on traditions of computing in computing education, a chapter on the standards for computer education, and a chapter on the application of the framework of technological pedagogical content knowledge for the teaching of spreadsheets. Each one of these chapters provides a framework that helps the reader to better understand, plan, arrange and manage the teaching of computer science.

Preliminary versions of four chapters in this book were presented during the ISDTF conference that was organized by the Serbian Academy of Sciences and Arts in 2011.

We hope that the reader will benefit from reading this book in many educational and professional ways.

The Editors

ACKNOWLEDGEMENT

The editors acknowledge financial support received from the Serbian Academy of Sciences and Arts, the Serbian Ministry of Education, Science and Technological Development (projects OI-174012 and III-44006), University of Cyprus, and Freie Universität Berlin. The editors also gratefully appreciate continuous support and encouragement from Alex Masulis, a senior Routledge editor, from the very early stages of this book to its completion and publication date.

CONTRIBUTORS

Charoula Angeli, *Department of Education, University of Cyprus, Cyprus*

Peter K. Antonitsch, *Institute for Informatics Systems/Didactics of Informatics, Alpen-Adria-Universität Klagenfurt, Austria*

Mikko Apiola, *Department of Computer Science, University of Helsinki, Finland*

Tim Bell, *Department of Computer Science and Software Engineering, University of Canterbury, New Zealand*

Mordechai Ben-Ari, *Department of Science Teaching, Weizmann Institute of Science, Israel*

Valentina Dagiene, *Institute of Mathematics and Informatics, Vilnius University, Lithuania*

Alexandra Gasparinatou, *Department of Informatics and Telecommunications, National and Kapodistrian University of Athens, Greece*

Maria Grigoriadou, *Department of Informatics and Telecommunications, National and Kapodistrian University of Athens, Greece*

Djordje M. Kadijevich, *Mathematical Institute, Serbian Academy of Sciences and Arts, and Faculty of Biofarming, Megatrend University, Serbia*

Heidi Newton, *School of Engineering and Computer Science, Victoria University of Wellington, New Zealand*

Mara Saeli, *Department of Computer Science Education, Freie Universität Berlin, Germany*

Carsten Schulte, *Department of Computer Science Education, Freie Universität Berlin, Germany*

Bronius Skupas, *Institute of Mathematics and Informatics, Vilnius University, Lithuania*

Matti Tedre, *Department of Computer and Systems Sciences, Stockholm University, Sweden*

PART 1

IMPROVING LEARNING

TEXT COMPREHENSION IN COMPUTER SCIENCE EDUCATION

Maria Grigoriadou and Alexandra Gasparinatou

Text comprehension

Texts are an important tool for learning. Many students are poor readers or have difficulty understanding textbooks (Snow, 2003). "To optimize learning, should one make the comprehension process as easy as possible, or should one, as many educators insist, ensure that the learner participates actively and intentionally in the process of constructing the meaning of the text?" (Kintsch, 1998). Specifically, should the readers' task be facilitated by improving the comprehensibility of a text or should the readers' active involvement be increased by placing obstacles in their way? In the second case, what sort of obstacles will have beneficial effects on learning and under what conditions? The approach to this question has been the study of characteristics of the text, the characteristics of the individual reader and how these factors affect text comprehension.

A considerable number of empirical studies have been conducted to answer this question. Many of them have demonstrated that readers' background knowledge facilitates and enhances comprehension and learning (McNamara et al., 1996; Gasparinatou & Grigoriadou, 2010). These studies have also shown that readers with greater background knowledge express more interest in the reading material and use more effective reading strategies. Additionally, experts tend to put more effort into learning than novices (Tobias, 1994).

Text comprehension can also be facilitated and enhanced by rewriting poorly written texts to be more cohesive and to provide the reader with all the information needed for a good comprehension (Beyer, 1991; Britton & Gulgoz, 1991; McKeown et al., 1992). Text coherence refers to the extent to which a reader is able to understand the relations between ideas in a text. This is generally dependent on whether these relationships are explicit in the text.

Nevertheless, a cohesive text representation does not always result in better learning. Readers with relevant prior knowledge do not always use that knowledge for learning. They also tend to take the path of least resistance, and if they feel that they easily understand the text they read, they may neglect to activate relevant prior knowledge in order to form links between their knowledge and the new text. Thus, there exists an instructional need to stimulate reader activity (Kintsch, 1998). Consequently, the advantages found for facilitating the reading process by making text more cohesive and the disadvantages demonstrated for facilitating the learning process present contradictory findings.

The construction-integration model

The theoretical framework for this chapter is the construction-integration model for comprehension (Kintsch, 1998). The construction-integration model was an extension of earlier models of comprehension (Kintsch & van Dijk, 1978; van Dijk & Kintsch, 1983), primarily specifying computationally the role of prior knowledge during the comprehension process. According to this model, comprehension arises from an interaction and fusion between the text information and knowledge activated by the learner. The final product of this construction and integration process is referred to as the reader's mental representation of the text.

Levels of understanding

This model distinguishes several different levels in the mental representation of a text that readers construct. The mental representation is a unitary structure, but it is useful to distinguish between certain aspects of that structure. The levels of understanding that are most relevant for the purposes of this chapter are the text base and the situation model.

The text base consists of those elements and relationships that are directly derived from the text itself. To construct the text base, the reader needs syntactic and semantic (lexical) knowledge.

The situation description that a learner constructs on the basis of a text as well as prior knowledge and experience is called the situation model. A situation model is, therefore, a construction that integrates the text-base and relevant aspects of the learner's knowledge.

The distinction between the micro- and the macro-structure of a text is orthogonal to the text base and situation model distinction. While the micro-structure refers to local text properties, the macro-structure refers to the global organization of text.

A third distinction refers to the quality of each one of these structures. One may have a poor text base (micro or macro), perhaps because the text is poorly written or perhaps because the learner did not encode properly what was there.

According to Kintsch's (1998) model, many factors contribute to learning from text, but prior domain-specific knowledge and the building of a coherent situation model are the driving factors.

The measurement of learning

As the levels of understanding are not separate structures and the situation model, by definition, involves both the text base and long-term memory, a comprehension measure cannot exclusively tap into one level of understanding. Some measures are more indicative of text memory (e.g., recognition, text-based questions, and reproductive recall) whereas other measures are more sensitive to learning (e.g., bridging inference questions, recall elaborations, problem-solving tasks, and keyword sorting tasks).

The former are referred to as text base measures, because all that is required for good performance is a coherent text base understanding. The latter are referred to as situation model measures, because to perform well on them, the reader must form a well-integrated situation model of the text during the comprehension process (Kintsch, 1998; McNamara et al., 1996).

Text cohesion

The degree to which the concepts, ideas, and relationships with a text are explicit has been referred to as text cohesion, whereas the effect of text cohesion on readers' comprehension has been referred to as text coherence (Graesser, McNamara, & Louwerse, 2003; McNamara et al., 1996). Text coherence refers to the extent to which a reader is able to understand the relations between ideas in a text and this is generally dependent on whether these relationships are explicit in the text. Text cohesion is one of the important dimensions along which text varies. It is an objective feature of texts, an important factor to determine text coherence, which is a subjective psychological state of a reader (Graesser et al., 2003).

Research in text comprehension

In the domain of history, Britton and Gulgoz (1991) found that partici-

4

pants who read the cohesive texts had better recall of the material, and developed a better situation model than participants who read less cohesive texts. Voss and Ney Silfies (1996) found that learning from an expanded text was related to reading-comprehension skill, whereas learning from an unexpanded text was a function of prior knowledge. Vidal-Abarca, Martinez, and Gilabert (2000) found that cohesive texts helped learners to generate a deeper understanding of the texts. The positive impact of cohesive text has been replicated by Linderholm et al. (2000) and also by Gilabert, Martinez, and Vidal-Abarca (2005).

In the domain of biology, McNamara et al. (1996) found that readers who know little about the domain of the text benefit from a maximally cohesive text, whereas high-knowledge readers benefit from a minimally cohesive text. Similarly, McNamara and Kintsch (1996) found that less cohesive text was more helpful for high-knowledge readers when they were asked questions, which revealed their understanding of the material (e.g., keyword sorting problem or open-ended questions asked after a delay). McNamara (2001) found that the low-cohesion advantage for learners of high-knowledge manifested at the text base model level. Ozuru, Dempesey, and McNamara (2009) found that (a) reading a high-cohesion text improved text-based comprehension, (b) overall comprehension was positively correlated with participants' prior knowledge, and (c) skilled participants gained more from high-cohesion text. In the domain of physics, Boscolo and Mason (2003) found that high-knowledge readers benefited from a minimally cohesive text.

In the domain of computer science, Beyer (1991) used a computer manual as his learning material. He revised the original manual by making its macro-structure explicit. The revised text proved to be significantly improved compared with the original version, but the improvement was restricted to problem-solving tasks. There is a lack of studies concerning learning from computer science texts. Computer science texts differ from those in social and natural sciences due to the following reasons (ACM & IEEE, 2008):

- Computer science texts are complex depending on factors mainly inherent in the texts. Much of their content is abstract and technical, far removed from everyday experience.
- Texts in computer science require students to utilize concepts from many different fields. All computer science students must learn to integrate theory and practice, to recognize the importance of abstraction, and to appreciate the value of good engineering design.

- Computer science texts assist students to develop a high level of understanding systems as a whole.

- Computer science texts must help students to encounter many recurring themes such as abstraction, complexity, and evolutionary change. They must also assist them to encounter principles (i.e., those associated with caching such as the principle of locality), with sharing a common resource, and so on.

Consequently, the way in which cohesion manipulations influence the comprehension and consequently the learning of computer science texts (e.g., computer networks texts) may differ from that of social and natural science texts. For the reasons mentioned above, we conducted two studies. In our first study (Gasparinatou & Grigoriadou, 2010), we investigated the effects of background knowledge on learning from high- and low-cohesion texts in the domain of computer science. The comprehension of 58 undergraduate students was examined in the domain of local network topologies using four versions of a text, orthogonally varying local and global cohesion. Participants' comprehension was examined through free-recall measure, text-based, elaborative-inference, bridging-inference and problem-solving questions, and a sorting task. The results showed that students with low and high background knowledge performed better with a high- and a low-cohesion text respectively, which implies adjusting text cohesion level to students' background knowledge.

In our second study (Gasparinatou & Grigoriadou, 2011a), we examined whether high-knowledge readers in computer science benefit from a text of low cohesion. Undergraduate students ($n = 65$) read one of four versions of a text concerning local network topologies, orthogonally varying local and global cohesion. Participants' comprehension was examined through free-recall measure, text-based, bridging-inference, elaborative-inference, problem-solving questions, and a sorting task. The results indicated that high-knowledge readers benefited from the low-cohesion text. The interaction of text cohesion and knowledge was reliable for the sorting activity, for elaborative-inference and for problem-solving questions. Although high-knowledge readers performed better in text-based and in bridging-inference questions with the low-cohesion text, the interaction of text cohesion and knowledge was not reliable. The results suggest a more complex view of when and for whom textual cohesion affects comprehension and consequently learning in computer science. These results also support the hypothesis that a text that requires gap-filling inferences is beneficial for learning in computer science.

Supporting comprehension with
personalized learning environments

There is a growing literature of studies focusing on assisting comprehension through personalized learning environments. In the early 1990s, the system Point&Query (P&Q), a hypertext/hypermedia system, was developed (Graesser, Langston, & Bagget, 1993). Students learned entirely by asking questions and interpreting answers to questions. In order to ask a question, the learner would point to a hot spot on the display by clicking a mouse. Then a list of questions would be presented. Thus, the learner could ask a question very easily, by two quick clicks of a mouse. On the average, a learner ends up asking 120 questions per hour, which is approximately 700 times the rate of questions in the classroom. The learner also is exposed to good questions because high-quality questions are presented on the menu of question options. Evaluations of the P&Q software asking revealed, however, that it is not sufficient to simply expose the students to a series of questions associated with hot spots in a large landscape of hypertext/hypermedia content. When participants are left to surf the hyperspace on their own, they tend to drift toward posing shallow questions. That is, the percentage of the learner's P&Q choices that were shallow questions was higher than chance among the questions available in the hyperspace (Graesser et al., 1993). The original P&Q software was developed for the subject matter of woodwind instruments and was suitable for high school and college students (Graesser, McNamara, & VanLehn, 2005).

AutoTutor is a computer tutor that attempts to stimulate the dialogue moves of a human tutor (Graesser et al., 2004; Graesser, Person, & Harter, 2001; Graesser, VanLehn, Rose, Jordan, & Harter, 2001). AutoTutor holds a conversation in natural language that coaches the student in constructing a good explanation in an answer, that corrects misconceptions, and that answers student questions. AutoTutor delivers its dialogue moves with an animated conversational agent that has a text-to-speech engine, facial expressions, gestures, and pointing. One goal of the tutor is to coach the student in covering the list of ten expectations. A second goal is to correct misconceptions that are manifested in the students' talk by simply correcting the errors as soon as they are manifested. A third goal is to adaptively respond to the student by giving short feedback on the quality of student contributions (positive, negative, or neutral) and by answering the student's questions. A fourth goal is to manage the dialogue in a fashion that appears coherent and accommodates unusual speech acts by learners. AutoTutor has been evaluated on learning gains in several experiments on the topics of computer literacy (Graesser et al., 2004) and conceptual physics (VanLehn et al., 2005). The results of these studies have been quite positive (Graesser et al., 2005).

MetaTutor is a hypermedia learning environment that is designed to detect, model, trace, and foster students' self-regulated learning about human body systems such as the circulatory, digestive, and nervous systems (Azevedo, 2008, 2009). Theoretically, it is based on cognitive models of self-regulated learning (Pintrich, 2000; Schunk, 2005; Winne & Hadwin, 2008; Zimmerman, 2001). The underlying assumption of MetaTutor is that students should regulate key cognitive and metacognitive processes in order to learn about complex and challenging science topics (Graesser et al., 2005).

SimStudents, an integrated learner model for history and equation problem solving, uses an ACT-R based cognitive model (MacLaren & Koedinger, 2002). Other systems include the Empirical Assessment of Comprehension (Mathan & Koedinger, 2002) and the model of comprehension and recall that is based on Trabasso and Van den Broek's model (Fletcher, van den Broek, & Arthur, 1996). In this model, the reader, in order to understand the text, has to find the causal path that links the text from the beginning to the end. Recently, various approaches have been proposed (Zapata-Riviera & Greer, 2002), which involve learners in negotiating dialogues, as well as learner models that encourage inspection and modification of the model.

W-ReTuDis (Web-Reflective Tutorial Dialogue System) is a web-based open learner modeling system designed to support tutorial dialogue through reflective learning. It models human diagnosis of learner's cognitive profile and constructs the learner model of historical text comprehension. The learner model is open for inspection, discussion, and negotiation. The system promotes learners' personalized reflection through tutorial dialogue, helps learners to be aware of their reasoning, and leads them toward scientific thought. The system offers a two-level open interactive environment: learner level and tutor level. In learner level, the learner participates in the construction of his/her learner model through dialogue activities, which promote reflective learning. In tutor level, the tutor based on the learner model makes decisions concerning the appropriate activity, reflective dialogue and dialogue strategy for the learner. The evaluation results are encouraging for the system's educational impact on the learners (Tsaganou & Grigoriadou, 2009).

iSTART (Interactive Strategy Training for Active Reading and Thinking) is a web-based tutoring program that uses animated agents to teach reading strategies to young adolescent (Grades 8–12) and college-aged students. The program is based on a live intervention called Self-Explanation Reading Training (SERT) that teaches metacognitive reading strategies in the context of self-explanation. SERT was motivated in the context of self-explanation. SERT was motivated too by empirical findings that students who self-explain text develop a deeper understanding of the concepts covered in text, combined with a large body of research showing the importance of reading strategies such as comprehension monitoring, making inferences, and elaboration. SERT was designed to improve self-explanation by teaching reading strategies and in turn to facilitate the learning of reading strategies in the context of self-explanation. SERT has been found to successfully improve students' comprehension and course performance at both the college and high school levels. iSTART was designed to deliver an automated version of SERT that could be more widely available and could adapt training to the needs of the student. The research has shown that SERT is most beneficial for students with the least knowledge about the domain as well as the students who are less strategic or less skilled readers. In this line of research, we developed the learning environment ALMA (Adaptive Learning Models from texts and Activities), which will be presented in the following section (Gasparinatou & Grigoriadou, 2011b).

An outline of the ALMA environment

ALMA actively engages students in the learning process. It takes into account readers' background knowledge in order to propose the appropriate text version from four versions of a text with the same content, but different cohesion at the local and global level. To achieve this goal, it suggests that the student performs a background knowledge assessment test, with scores characterized as "high," "median," and "low." ALMA motivates high-knowledge students to read the minimally cohesive text at both local and global levels (lg), median-knowledge students to read the text with maximum local and minimum global cohesion (Lg) or the text with minimum local and maximum global cohesion (lG), and low-knowledge students to read the maximally cohesive text (LG). ALMA also allows the student to choose the preferred version of text and records the time spent reading it. The following three types of rules were used to maximize local cohesion: (1) Replacing pronouns with noun phrases when the referent was potentially ambiguous (e.g., in the phrase *"This has been very popular for exchanging music files via the internet,"* we replace *"This"* by *"The peer-to-*

peer model"). (2) Adding descriptive elaborations linking unfamiliar and familiar concepts (e.g., the sentence *"In networks, computers users can exchange messages and share resources"* was changed to: *"In networks, computers users can exchange messages and share resources, such as printing capabilities, software packages, and data storage facilities that are scattered throughout the system"*). (3) Adding sentence connectives (i.e., however, therefore, because, so that) to specify the relation between sentences or ideas. In the global macro cohesion versions of the texts (lG and LG), macro propositions were signaled explicitly by various linguistic means (i.e., macro signals), such as, (a) adding topic headers (e.g., Network Classifications, Protocols), and (b) adding macro propositions serving to link each paragraph to the rest of the text and the overall topic (e.g., *"Afterwards, the rules by which network activities are conducted, will be discussed"*).

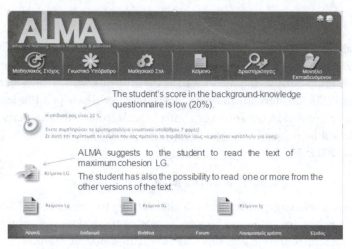

Fig. 1. ALMA suggests the appropriate text to the student

ALMA supports and assesses students' comprehension through a series of activities such as: text recall, summaries, text-based questions, bridging inference, elaborative inference, problem solving, case studies, active experimentation, and sorting tasks. *Text recall* helps students remember the basic ideas in the text by translating it into more familiar words. The students are also encouraged to go beyond the basic sentence-focused processing by linking the content of the sentences to other information, either from the text or from the students' background knowledge. The empirical findings have shown that students who are able to recall the text and go beyond the basic sentence-focused processing are more successful at solving problems, more likely to generate inferences, construct more coherent mental models, and develop a deeper understanding of the concepts covered in the text (Chi et al., 1994) (e.g., *"Describe in your own words the operation of network based on client-server model"*). *Summaries* also encourage students to go beyond the text and like text recall can be perfectly good indicators of well-developed situation models (Kintsch, 1998) (e.g., *"Describe briefly the ways in which networks are interconnected"*). As they demand only a specific detail from the text, *text-based questions* measure text memory (e.g., *"Which device is used to connect two incompatible networks?"*).

Bridging-inferences questions motivate students to make *bridging inferences,* which improve comprehension by linking the current sentence to the material previously covered in the text (e.g., Oakhill, 1984). Such inferences allow the reader to form a more cohesive global representation of the text content (Kintsch, 1998) (e.g., *"Compare the advantages and disadvantages between networks based on client-server model and on peer-to-peer model"*). *Elaborative-inference questions* motivate students to associate the current sentence with their own related background knowledge. The most important is that students are encouraged to engage in logical or analogical reasoning process to relate the content of the sentence with domain-general knowledge or any experiences related to the subject matter, particularly when they do not have sufficient knowledge about the topic of the text.

Research has established that both domain knowledge and elaborations based on more general knowledge are associated with improving learning and comprehension (Pressley et al., 1992). *Elaborations* essentially ensure that the information in the text is linked to information that the reader already knows. These connections to background knowledge result in a more coherent and stable representation of the text content (Kintsch, 1998; McNamara et al., 1996) (e.g., *"Could the internet function properly if we replaced the routers with bridges?"*). In order to answer this question, the student has to link the information in the text with the information from background knowledge.

Problem-solving questions motivate students to use the information acquired from the text productively in novel environments. This requires that the text information be integrated with the students' background knowledge and become a part of it, so that it can support comprehension and problem solving in new situations (Kintsch, 1998) (e.g., *"In the following figure, the nodes 01 and 02 consist the network 1 whereas the nodes 03, 04, 05, and 06 consist the network 2. The two networks are interconnected with a bridge. Let's assume that the node 03 intends to send a message to node 02. Describe the process which will be followed").*

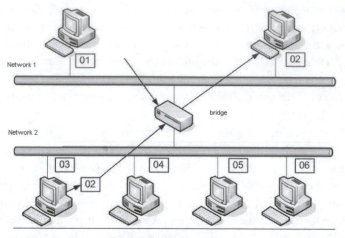

Fig. 2. Delivery of a message

Case studies motivate students to engage in the solution of an authentic and thus interesting problem. They are asked to analyze it and propose solutions (Pyatt, 2006). The problem is described in detail and is followed by a series of questions aiming to guide the students in the procedure of problem solving (e.g., *Students are given to study the process of mission and reception of a message. Then they are given the solution and clarifications about the solution of the problem*).

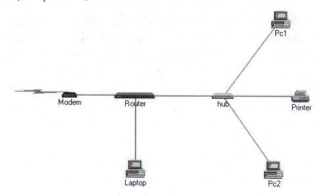

Fig. 3. A home network

Active experimentation activities motivate students to undertake an active role and through experimentation to construct their own internal representations for the concept they are studying (e.g., *Students are given the diagram of a home network (Fig. 3) and they are asked if the network oper-*

ates properly. Next, they are asked to design the same network by themselves via a software tool (e.g., Network Notepad) and check via the software if their original answer was correct).

A *sorting task* has great potential as a simple task and can be used both as a method of assessment and as a mode of instruction. Students are asked to sort a set of key words, contained and not contained in the text, in certain groups. They are encouraged to do this task twice, once before reading the text and once more after reading the text. The sorting data are used to determine the influence of the text in students' conceptual structure. We are interested in the degree to which the information presented in the text influences their sorting. A sorting task is an alternative method for assessing situation model understanding (e.g., *"Sort each of the following concepts: client server, administrator, in one of the following categories: client-server model, peer-to-peer model, distributed systems"*).

Afterwards, they are given a similar problem concerning the web-based game "World of Warcraft," which exploits the internet and specifically the client-server model, and it permits us to play in a virtual environment with an agent. There are also other users in this environment with whom we are able to chat when they are on line or send them a message. Next, students are asked to describe the process that will be followed in order for a user to connect with the specific network and to communicate with another user when the other user is either on line or off line.

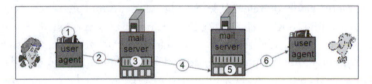

Fig. 4. The route of data in the network

Moreover ALMA supports multiple Informative, Tutoring, and Reflective Feedback Components aiming to stimulate learners to reflect on their beliefs, to guide and tutor them towards the achievement of specific learning outcomes, and to inform them about their performance (Gouli et al., 2005) (e.g., *"Your answer is correct!"* or *"Your answer is not correct!"* or *"You may have to read again carefully the paragraph concerning the peer-to-peer model"*).

ALMA also actively engages students in the learning process by taking into account readers' learning preferences in order to propose to them to start from activities that match their learning preferences and continue with less learning preferences matched activities in order to develop new capabilities (Kolb, 1984). To achieve this goal, it suggests that the student performs the learning style inventory (LSI; Kolb, 1993). LSI describes the way a student learns and how he/she deals with ideas and day-to-day situations in his/her life. It includes 12 sentences with a choice of endings. Consequently, ALMA is adapted to students' background knowledge and learning style resulting in personalized learning.

ALMA also includes the authoring tool ALMA_auth, which provides the author with the option of developing and uploading educational material. Finally, ALMA includes a forum where students have the possibility to collaborate with each other and also with the instructor. The learner model in ALMA keeps information about (a) learners' background knowledge level and learning style, and (b) learners' behavior during interaction with the environment in terms of the learning sequence chosen, time spent on reading the text, time spent on an activity, etc.

Educational implications

The cohesion of a text from which a student is supposed to acquire knowledge is very important. When comprehending a text, readers must establish and maintain coherence between sentences (Oakhill, Cain, & Bryant, 2003). When reading a highly cohesive text, the majority of information necessary to maintain text coherence is provided by the text itself. On the other hand, when reading a less cohesive text, readers need to rely more heavily on relevant knowledge to maintain coherence.

According to Kintsch (1998), there is no text comprehension that does not require the reader to apply knowledge: lexical, syntactic, and semantic knowledge, domain knowledge, personal experience, and so on. Ideally, a text should contain the new information a reader needs to know plus just enough old information to allow the reader to link the new information with what is already known. Texts that contain too much that the reader already knows are boring to read and, indeed, confusing (e.g., legal and insurance documents that leave nothing to be taken for granted). Consequently, too much coherence and explication may not necessarily be a good thing.

In short, comprehension may not succeed equally well at all levels, such as the text base or the situation model. If comprehension proceeds well at the level of the text base (e.g., for a high-knowledge reader with a cohesive text), the student may fail to work harder for a deeper understanding. With respect to educational applications, our findings suggest an approach in which the cohesion level of the text is adjusted to the students' level of knowledge, so that reading becomes challenging enough to stimulate active processing but not so difficult as to break down comprehension.

This would mean constructing several versions of a text in order to accommodate varying levels of knowledge among readers. This educational application of customized text is achievable within the capability of present-day hypertext computer systems. Instructional text could be presented at the level of cohesion that is appropriate to the student's current level of understanding.

In the domain of computer science, ALMA applies this approach and supports and assesses students' comprehension through a series of activities. In this way, students are supported to use their knowledge as they read, allowing effective learning to be achieved by a much wider range of students than is possible with a single text targeted at a supposed average reader. ALMA also supports students with activities corresponding to different levels of comprehension, which prompt the student to practically implement different text-reading strategies, with the recommended activity sequence adapted to the student's learning style.

Digital learning material, in accordance with the text comprehension model described by Kintsch (1998), was introduced into the ALMA environment. The material includes texts of varying local and global cohesion and activities corresponding to different comprehension levels and appropriate for all learning styles. This material can be exploited in either distance or blended learning. The assessment of ALMA demonstrated that the ALMA environment satisfactorily supported the learning process of students in computer science and almost all its functions are useful and user-friendly.

References

ACM and IEEE. (2008). *Computer science. Curriculum 2008: An interim revision of CS 2001. Report from the Interim Review Task Force*. Association for Computing Machinery and the IEEE Computer Society.

Azevedo, R. (2009). Theoretical, conceptual, methodological, and instructional issues in research on metacognition and self-regulated learning: A discussion. *Metacognition and Learning*, 4(1), 87–95.

Azevedo, R. (2008). The role of self-regulation in learning about science with hypermedia. In D. Robinson & G. Schraw (Eds.), *Recent innovations in educational technology that facilitate student learning* (pp. 127–156). Charlotte, NC: Information Age Publishing.

Beyer, R. (1991). Psychologische Untersuchungen zur Gestaltung von Instruktionstexten. *Mathematisch-Naturwissenschaftliche Reihe*, 39(1), 69–75.

Boscolo, P., & Mason, L. (2003). Topic knowledge, text coherence, and interest: How they interact in learning from instructional texts. *Journal of Experimental Education*, 71(2), 126–148.

Britton, B. K., & Gulgoz, S. (1991). Using Kintsch's computational model to improve instructional text: Effects of repairing inferences calls on recall and cognitive structures. *Journal of Educational Psychology, 83*(3), 329–345.

Chi, M. T. H., de Leeuw, N., Chiu, M., & LaVancher, C. (1994). Eliciting self-explanations improves understanding. *Cognitive Science, 18*(3), 439–477.

Fletcher, C., van den Broek, P., & Arthur, E. (1996). A model of narrative comprehension and recall. In B. Britton & C. Graesser (Eds.), *Models of Understanding Text* (pp. 230–241). Mahwah, NJ: Erlbaum.

Gasparinatou, A., & Grigoriadou, M. (2011a). Supporting students' learning in the domain of Computer Science. *Computer Science Education, 21*(1), 1–28.

Gasparinatou, A., & Grigoriadou, M. (2011b). ALMA: An Adaptive Learning Models environment from texts and Activities that improves students' science comprehension. *Procedia-Social and Behavioral Sciences Journal, 15*, 2742–2747.

Gasparinatou, A., & Grigoriadou, M. (2010). Learning from texts in computer science. *The International Journal of Learning, 17*(1), 171–189 .

Gilabert, R., Martinez, G., & Vidal-Abarca, E. (2005). Some texts are always better: Text revision to foster inferences of readers with high and low background knowledge. *Learning and Instruction, 15*(1), 45–68.

Gouli, E., Gogoulou, A., Papanikolaou, K., & Grigoriadou, M. (2005). An adaptive feedback framework to support reflection, guiding and tutoring. In G. Magoulas & S. Chen (Eds.), *Advances in web-based education: Personalized learning environments* (pp. 178–202). Hershey, PA: Idea Group.

Graesser, A. C., Langston, M. C., & Baggett, W. B. (1993). Exploring information about concepts by asking questions. In G. V. Nakamura, R. M. Taraban, & D. Medin (Eds.), *The psychology of learning and motivation: Categorization by humans and machines* (pp. 411–436). Orlando, FL: Academic Press.

Graesser, A. C., Lu, S., Jackson, G. T., Mitchell, H., Ventura, M., Olney, A., & Louwerse, M. M. (2004). AutoTutor: A tutor with dialogue in natural language. *Behavioral Research Methods, Instruments, and Computers, 36*(2), 180–192.

Graesser, A. C., McNamara, D. S., & Louwerse, M. M. (2003). What do readers need to learn in order to process coherence relations in narrative and expository text? In A. P. Sweet & C. E. Snow (Eds.), *Rethinking reading comprehension* (pp. 82–98). New York: Guilford Publications.

Graesser, A. C., McNamara, D. S., & VanLehn, K. (2005). Scaffolding deep comprehension strategies through Point&Query, AutoTutor, and iSTART. *Educational Psychologist, 40*(4), 225–234.

Graesser, A. C., Person, N. K., Harter, D. (2001). Teaching tactics and dialogue in AutoTutor. *International Journal of Artificial Intelligence in Education, 12*(3), 257–279.

Graesser, A. C., VanLehn, K., Rose, C., Jordan, P., & Harter, D. (2001). Intelligent tutoring systems with conversational dialogue. *AI Magazine, 22*(4), 39–51.

Kintsch, W. (1998). *Comprehension: A paradigm for cognition.* Cambridge: Cambridge University Press.

Kintsch, W., & van Dijk, T. A. (1978). Towards a model of text comprehension and production. *Psychological Review, 85*(5), 363–394.

Kolb, D. A. (1993). *LSI-IIa: Self scoring inventory and interpretation booklet.* Boston: McBer & Company.

Kolb, D. A. (1984). *Experiential learning.* Englewood Cliffs, NJ: Prentice-Hall.

Linderholm, T., Everson, M., van den Broek, P., Mischinski, M., Crittenden, A., & Samuels, J. (2000). Effects of causal text revisions on more- and less-skilled readers' comprehension of easy and difficult texts. *Cognition and Instruction, 18*(4), 525–556.

Mathan, S., & Koedinger, R., (2002). An empirical assessment of comprehension fostering features in an intelligent system. In S. A. Cerri, G. Gouardères, & F. Paraguaçu (Eds.), *Intelligent tutoring systems* (pp. 330–343). *Lecture Notes in Computer Science*, Vol. 2363. Berlin: Springer.

McKeown, M. G., Beck, I. L., Sinatra, G. M., & Loxterman, J. A. (1992). The contribution of prior knowledge and coherent text to comprehension. *Reading Research Quarterly, 27*(1), 79–93.

McLaren, B., & Koedinger, K. (2002). When and why does mastery learning work: Instructional experiments with ACT-R "SimStudents". In S. A. Cerri, G. Gouardères, & F. Paraguaçu (Eds.), *Intelligent tutoring systems* (pp. 355–366). *Lecture Notes in Computer Science*, Vol. 2363. Berlin: Springer.

McNamara, D. S. (2001). Reading both high-coherence and low-coherence texts: Effects of text sequence and prior knowledge. *Canadian Journal of Experimental Psychology, 55*(1), 51–62.

McNamara, D. S., & Kintsch, W. (1996). Learning from texts: Effects of prior knowledge and text coherence. *Discourse Processes, 22*(3), 247–288.

McNamara, D. S., Kintsch, E., Songer, N. B., & Kintsch, W. (1996). Are good texts always better? Text coherence, background knowledge, and levels of understanding in learning from text. *Cognition and Instruction, 14*(1), 1–43.

Oakhill, J. (1984). Inferential and memory skills in children's comprehension of stories. *British Journal of Educational Psychology, 54*(1), 31–39.

Oakhill, J. V., Cain. K., & Bryant, P. E. (2003). Dissociation of single-word reading and text comprehension skills. *Language and Cognitive Processes, 18*(4), 443–468.

Ozuru, Y., Dempesey, K., & McNamara D. S. (2009). Prior knowledge, reading skill, and text cohesion in the comprehension of science texts. *Learning and Instruction, 19*(3), 228–242.

Pyatt, E. J. (2006). Using cases in teaching. *Teaching and learning with technology*. Penn State University. Retrieved December 10, 2012, from archive.tlt.psu.edu/suggestions/cases/

Pintrich, P. (2000). The role of goal orientation in self-regulated learning. In M. Boekaerts, P. Pintrich, & M. Zeidner (Eds.), *Handbook of self-regulation* (pp. 451–502). San Diego, CA: Academic Press.

Pressley, M., Wood, E., Woloshyn, V., Martin, V., King, A., & Menke, D. (1992). Encouraging mindful use of prior knowledge: Attempting to construct explanatory answers facilitates learning. *Educational Psychology, 27*(1), 91–109.

Schunk, D. (2005). Self-regulated learning: The educational legacy of Paul R. Pintrich. *Educational Psychologist, 40*(2), 85–94.

Snow, C. E. (2003). Assessment of reading comprehension. In A. P. Sweet & C. E. Snow (Eds.), *Rethinking reading comprehension* (pp. 192–218). New York: Guilford.

Tobias, S. (1994). Interest, prior knowledge, and learning. *Review of Educational Research, 64*(1), 37–54.

Tsaganou, G., & Grigoriadou, M. (2009). Design of text comprehension activities with RE-TUDISAuth. In S. Pinder (Ed.), *Advances in human-computer interaction* (pp. 161–172). Vienna, Austria: I-Tech Education and Publishing.

van Dijk, T.A., & Kintsch, W. (1983). *Strategies of discourse comprehension*. New York: Academic Press.

VanLehn, K., Graesser, A. C., Jackson, G. T., Jordan, P., Olney, A., & Rose, C. P. (2005). When is reading just as effective as one-on-one interactive human tutoring? In B. G. Bara, L. Barsalou, & M. Bucciarelli (Eds.), *Proceedings of the 27th Annual Conference of the Cognitive Science Society* (pp. 2259–2264). Mahwah, NJ: Erlbaum.

Vidal-Abarca, E., Martinez,G., & Gilabert, R. (2000). Two procedures to improve instructional text: Effects on memory and learning. *Journal of Educational Psychology, 92*(1), 107–116.

Voss, J. F., & Silfies, L. N. (1996). Learning from history text: The interaction of knowledge and comprehension skill with text structure. *Cognition and Instruction, 14*(1), 45–68.

Winne, P., & Hadwin, A. (2008). The weave of motivation and self-regulated learning. In D. Schunk & B. Zimmerman (Eds.), *Motivation and self-regulated learning: Theory, research, and applications* (pp. 297–314). New York: Taylor & Francis.

Zapata-Riviera, J. D., & Greer, J. (2002). Exploring various guidance mechanisms to support interaction with inspectable learner models. In S. A. Cerri, G. Gouardères, & F. Para-guaçu (Eds.), *Intelligent tutoring systems* (pp. 442–452). *Lecture Notes in Computer Science*, Vol. 2363. Berlin: Springer.

Zimmerman, B. (2001). Investigating self-regulation and motivation: Historical background, methodological developments, and future prospects. *Review of Educational Research, 45*(1), 166–183.

2

LEARNING ABOUT
SPREADSHEETS

Djordje M. Kadijevich

Introduction

Computerized spreadsheets have been used in business for about 30 years. They are today, for example, major tools in the finance industry (Croll, 2005), most financial documents and many management reports being in that form.

Despite the relevance of spreadsheets to today's workplace, research in computer science education has neglected these versatile modeling tools. An examination of various bibliographic databases done by the author of this chapter in December 2012, by using the word *spreadsheet* for article titles, revealed the following data:

- There are only two such papers in the proceedings of *ISSEP* (Informatics in School: Situation, Evolution, and Perspective) conferences published by Springer (one paper was published in 2005, other in 2008).
- There is just one paper published in a Routledge journal *Computer Science Education*.
- Although there are seven such papers published in an ACM journal *SIGCSE Bulletin*, none of them has been published in the last seven years. Note that, for example, *Interfaces*, a journal on issues of operations research and management sciences, had a special issue on spreadsheets in 2008 (see http://interfaces.journal.informs.org/).

The previous paragraph clearly evidences that researchers in computer science education have had little interest in studying issues associated with developing and using spreadsheets. Why is this so? Some findings of the *DidaTab* project, a French project on the personal and classroom use of spreadsheets, offers an answer. It was found that this neglect of spreadsheets was probably the result of a widespread view that: (1) there are no interesting problems related to spreadsheets, and (2) teaching spreadsheets is not necessary because spreadsheet learning occurs naturally through practice (for more details, visit www.stef.ens-cachan.fr/didatab/en/summary.htm).

There are interesting and important spreadsheet-related problems in both practice and research. Aiming to improve spreadsheet learning, this chapter examines lessons learned from both professional practice and an educational context. On the basis of these lessons, the chapter ends with implications for teacher education.

Spreadsheets in business context

This part comprises three sections. The first section deals with errors in operational spreadsheets, their financial impact, and sources of these errors. The second section summarizes the present state of spreadsheet management and indicates main activities that would improve it. The third and last section gives implications for spreadsheet learning.

Spreadsheet errors, their financial impact, and sources of them

Operational spreadsheets that are in day-to-day use in organizations are quite prone to errors. The internet presentation of *EuSpRIG* (European Spreadsheets Risk Interest Group), for example, contains many case studies, mainly with errors in formulas (examine www.eusprig.org/horror-stories.htm). It was an uncontrolled use of spreadsheets in the credit derivatives marketplace that contributed substantially to the recent destruction of the capital of the global financial system (Croll, 2009).

A 2009 *PricewaterhouseCoopers* report underlined that "95% of the Excel spreadsheets examined had errors out of which 80% had significant monetary errors" ("Spreadsheet mistakes," 2009; p. 1). According to Powell, Baker, and Lawson (2009a), errors were present in about 1–2% of all formulas used. The most frequent error was using formulas with incorrect reference(s) to other cells (48.8% of all errors generating wrong results). Other errors were wrong formulas (31.7%), placing numbers in formulas (11%), and using missing or wrong data (3.6%). [Although, at first sight, nothing is wrong with placing a number in a formula when this number is correct (e.g. =0.18*C16; assume that tax rate at present is 18%), it may be (quite) error-prone to go from formula to formula to locate the number and change its value because it may be the value of another business element as well.]

Spreadsheet errors may have serious financial consequences. Powell,

Baker, and Lawson (2009b) audited 25 operational spreadsheets. In doing so, they found 117 errors confirmed by their developers. Although 47 errors (about 40%) did not have financial consequences, 27 of the remaining 70 errors had an impact of at least $100,000 (with seven of them with an impact of $10,000,000 or more). Some of the examined spreadsheets were used in a big financial firm, which calculated large tax liabilities. "These [tax liability] spreadsheets were astonishingly complex, difficult to understand, difficult to work with, and error-prone" (*ibid*, p. 131). Because a $100,000 error may be marginal in one spreadsheet and catastrophic in another, the relative impact of the confirmed errors was also reported in Powell, Baker, and Lawson (2009b). They found that sixteen errors were more than 10% of the initial value, with four 100%+ errors.

Powell, Baker, and Lawson (2008) found that spreadsheet errors can, in general, be attributed to the use of a wrong model, function attribute, or data. The main reasons for these errors could be found in (1) using a chaotic spreadsheet design, (2) entering numbers in formulas, (3) determining similar results in different ways, (4) using formulas in a row or a column that have different structures, and (5) using complex formulas. The reasons that spreadsheet developers did not develop better models might primarily be found in (a) applying an unstructured spreadsheet design, (b) changing the requirements of the model under development, (c) working under excessive time pressure, (d) lack of any formal testing, and (e) lack of relevant knowledge and skills regarding the modeling tool or the problem domain (Powell, Baker, & Lawson, 2009b).

Spreadsheet management and its improvement

Most spreadsheet developers and users are self-taught (e.g., Croll, 2005). Bearing in mind the frequency of spreadsheet errors and their financial impacts, there is a need for not only good spreadsheet education, but also company standards for developing and using spreadsheets as well as measuring spreadsheet errors (Hesse & Scerno, 2009).

Do companies evaluate and protect spreadsheets that are important to their business?

A recent business report from *Deloitte* ("Spreadsheet management," 2009) showed that although 70% of companies relied on spreadsheets for a critical portion of the business, just one-third of them used specialized techniques to control and manage spreadsheets. Spreadsheets were indeed included in a company's periodic risk assessment in many companies, but this nevertheless happened in less than half (42%) of them. These figures evidence that spreadsheet management is in a sad state at present.

As Kulesz (2011) underlined, there is no agreement on best practices for spreadsheets. Also, is not clear whether good, context-independent practices exist. However, the Delloite report mentioned above ("Spreadsheet management," 2009) proposes ongoing audit activities that would improve spreadsheet management. These activities comprise the following six steps: (1) identify the population of spreadsheets for review, (2) create a spreadsheet inventory, (3) rank each spreadsheet's risk level, (4) develop a baseline for each spreadsheet, (5) evaluate policies and procedures for spreadsheet use, and (6) review controls that protect spreadsheet baselines (these steps are listed on p. 3).

Step (4) is the central step in these activities, through which auditors test whether a spreadsheet is functioning according to management's intentions regarding input data and formulas. Because of that, good spreadsheet management should include (position tailored) support for employees in (a) understanding data and, if needed, questioning and improving their quality, (b) understanding (some) relationships in models and, if needed, questioning and improving these relationships, and (c) understanding models and, if needed, questioning and improving them (these three kinds of support are listed in Kadijevich, 2010, p. 318).

Because data quality is still poor today, support under (a) regarding this quality is equally important to support under (b) or (c). It was found, for example, that 42% of big companies from various industries did not measure or monitor data quality, whereas most of them (71%) underlined that maintaining good data quality was hard ("The state of data quality," 2009). As 39% of the sampled companies had annual revenues over one billion dollars, these are quite shocking findings that indeed flag a big business problem.

Implications for spreadsheet learning

Undoubtedly, spreadsheet learning should promote good practices for the development of spreadsheets and their applications. Having in mind the content of the two previous sections, this learning should care about (1) improving knowledge of the tool and the underlying mathematics, (2) using a structured spreadsheet design, (3) applying a detailed formal testing of spreadsheet developed, and (4) questioning the quality of data, formulas, and model used and improving them as needed.

Regarding knowledge of the tool, it can be improved, for example, through learning how to audit formulas in spreadsheet software, which is, for example, enabled in Microsoft Excel 2007. Of course, spreadsheet auditing in this software can also be done by using some add-ins, such as

Learning about spreadsheets

Spreadsheet Professional available at www.spreadsheetinnovations.com A screenshot given in Figure 1 shows how to audit a formula in the software and this add-in. Through auditing formulas, basic computing concepts (e.g., data types, variables, and functions) can be mastered and connected. Such learning, including the problem domain, can also be done through creating self-checks, which, for example, compare some critical ratios (e.g., marketing costs/production costs) from period to period, use different ways to determine the value of question, or use different scenarios to uncover problematic data (see O'Beirne, 2009, for such checks).

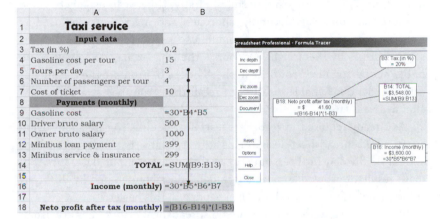

Fig. 1. Formula auditing

Using tools for auditing in a systematic way would promote learning that takes care of issues (3) and (4) mentioned above (applying a detailed formal testing of spreadsheet developed; questioning the quality of data, formulas, and model used and improving them as needed). Of course, the validity of data, formulas, and model cannot be determined by auditing tools; these can only help developers/auditors to uncover problematic issues, such as using poor or missing input data, applying correct functions wrongly, or using wrong functions. Regarding data quality, auditing tools can uncover, among other things, the differences between two data sets, suspicious data items, missing data items, and improperly formatted data (O'Beirne, 2008). Microsoft Excel 2007, for example, enables data quality auditing with several options, such as **Data / Data Validation** and **Home / Find & Select / Go To Special**. There are also add-ins for this program that deal with the quality of data, such as *ActiveData*. This versatile tool is available at www.informationactive.com, where the reader can find a number of short videos that demonstrate the use of the tool.

23

Can such videos improve the learning of computer science and when is this likely to happen?

Research shows the positive effects of the use of short videos of good programming practice in the teaching of programming, which may start from programs developed by students (Bennedsen & Caspersen, 2008). [These videos can easily be developed by using software for screen recording and movie making, such as *CamStudio* and *Windows Movie Maker*.] Using short videos of good auditing practices would improve spreadsheet learning provided that, as Tort (2010) stated, these videos go beyond doing things in a step-by-step fashion. Firstly, things can usually be done in more than one way. Secondly, shortcuts and macros may be used as well. Because of that, the videos should also support learners to develop some routines by themselves. Of course, the learner may document some of his/her personalized routines in short videos to promote the learning of other students or enable him/her to recall these routines at a later occasion in an easy way.

As already required, spreadsheet learning should also care about using a structured spreadsheet design. This at first means that each spreadsheet should be divided into separate areas that contain input data, intermediate results, output data, and check data, possibly denoted by different colors. What other things should be included in this design?

As underlined in the first section on spreadsheet errors, they are usually generated by (a) entering numbers in formulas, (b) using formulas in a row or a column that have different structures, and (c) using complex formulas. In order to attain a structured design, the developer should respect the opposite of (a), (b), and (c). Firstly, instead of having some numbers in formulas, he/she should put these numbers in the area for input data and only use formulas that contain the addresses of cells containing the numbers. Secondly, he/she should make use of a row or a column that contains formulas of the same structure (e.g., = B5*D11, = B5*D12, ... , = B5*D22), taking special care for cells whose addresses must be absolute (B5 in our example). Thirdly, he/she should break complex formula down into two or more chunks of calculations and take care with these intermediate results.

What can research on mathematics in the workplace contribute to the improvement of spreadsheet learning?

It was Steen (2003) who underlined a number of features of mathematics in the workplace including the following: (1) the workplace frequently typically requires a sophisticated application of just elementary mathematics, and (2) workplace calculations are rich in data and require a high degree of accuracy. He also underlined that these features are usually missing in traditional learning situations. Having in mind the notion of techno-mathematical literacy in the workplace (Hoyles et al., 2007), spreadsheet learning can implement the two features and their techno-mathematical prerequisites and results in good spreadsheet practice provided that it care about the mathematics involved in business models, computing concepts involved in spreadsheet modeling, the tools applied and their affordances, and the quality of data, formulas and models used.

Spreadsheets in educational context

This part, like the previous one, comprises three sections. The first section summarizes the outcomes of a study on spreadsheet errors focusing on error types and their frequencies, whereas the second section presents three studies that discussed sources of spreadsheet errors. The third and last section contains implications for spreadsheet learning.

Types of spreadsheet errors and their frequencies

One of the first studies on spreadsheet errors in detail, done in an educational context, was probably the one conducted by Teo and Tan (1999). Their study used a sample of second-year undergraduate students who developed spreadsheets within a course on information systems. These spreadsheets were developed to prepare a bid for building a wall, representing one business situation fully clarified with respect to the data the developers had to consider. This study examined qualitative and quantitative errors and found the following:

1) There were three quantitative errors: *omission errors* (e.g., forgetting to include the cost of materials in the expenses), *mechanical errors* (e.g., mistyping a number or using a wrong cell), and *logic errors* (e.g., calculating total costs by using variable costs only). Their relative frequencies (proportions) were about 15%, 15%, and 25%, respectively.

2) Poor spreadsheet design was the result of two qualitative errors: *jamming* (using formulas that contain numbers) and *duplication* (having the same datum or data at two or more places). There were about 4.5 such errors per spreadsheet developed; about 70% of them were jamming errors.

3) Mechanical errors were significantly negatively correlated with duplication errors, whereas logic errors were significantly positively correlated with jamming errors.

4) 'What-if' analysis, used to improve the developed models, helped the developers correct some errors but introduced many new ones: while

the number of new logic errors was similar to the number of logic errors corrected, the former number for mechanical and omission errors was greater than the latter one; although the number of new jamming errors was smaller than the number of jamming errors corrected, there were about five times more new duplication errors than duplication errors corrected.

Sources of spreadsheet errors

Being focused on sources of spreadsheet errors, Hoag (2008) applied a distinction between *domain knowledge* errors and *implementation* errors. It was assumed that a domain knowledge error was manifested when the spreadsheet developer used a wrong algorithm (real-world error) or a wrong formula in an appropriate algorithm (error in mathematical representation), whereas an implementation error was found in cases when he/she used a formula with wrong elements (syntax error) or an incorrectly constructed formula (logic error). [In determining income per product model (in %), for example, the developer might use a wrong formula =D9/D5 instead of the correct one =D5/D9 (committing an error in mathematical representation), or construct an incorrect formula =D5/D10 instead of the correct one =D5/D9 or =D5/D9 (committing a logic error). Of course, as in any categorization, some errors may be related to more than one category.] The participants in his study were college students who did simple spreadsheet modeling (e.g., determined the profit for a hypothetical company) by using starter templates similar to those represented in Figure 2. This modeling was based upon detailed specifications given to the students, such as: expenses for electricity were $300; cost of materials was 70% of the total income in cell D8; tax rate was: 15% for profit greater than $30,000, otherwise 12%. Despite such detailed specifications, the template support, and relatively simple formulas required (e.g., only with functions SUM, IF, and PMT), the students did make both domain knowledge errors and logic implementation errors. In other words, spreadsheet errors stemmed from a lack of domain knowledge as well as spreadsheet knowledge.

Tort, Blondel, and Bruillard (2008) is another study concerned with sources of spreadsheet errors. This study examined the spreadsheet competencies of French high school students by using a framework comprising the following five main categories: cell and sheets editing and formatting; formulas; graphs and charts; data tables; and modeling. It was found that all students had difficulties with tasks that involved a deeper knowledge of spreadsheet concepts and features. These difficulties were connected not only to a lack of informatics competencies, but also to an unskilled use of software interface. More specifically, students did not master concepts of variables, data types, data tables, and functions. They also did not master basic principles of software interface (e.g., selection-action procedure, automatic program behavior, definition of default parameters), which limited them to anticipate results of their interactions with software interface. [When, for example, a student uses the option *AutoSum*, the software automatically selects the whole range of cells and calculates the result, but the result may, as this selection of cells, simply be wrong.] These two sources of difficulties, informatics concepts incompetence and software interface principles incompetence, may be respectively used to explain (to some extent) errors in mathematical representation and logic errors examined by Hoag (2008). Although mathematical concepts of variables and functions, for example, appear in both mathematics and informatics (computer science), each of them is treated differently in these subjects.

	A	B	C	D
1	**Computer sales**			
2				
3	**Monthly income**			
4	Model	Number sold	Price	Income per model
5	light	60	$495	
6	standard	50	$795	
7	business	40	$1,295	
8			Total	
9				
10	**Mortgage**			
11		APR	Years	Amount	Monthly payment
12		5.00%	10	$200,000	
13				
14	**Monthly expenses**			
15	Mortgage			
16	Phone			
17	Electricity			
18	Payroll			
19	Cost of materials			
20	Other expenses			
21	**Total**			
22				
23	**Profit**			
24	Profit			
25	Tax rate			
26	Taxes			
27	Net profit			

	A	B	C	D	E	F	G	H
1	**Weekly payroll**					8%		
2								
3	EID	Name	Rate	Hours	Gross pay	Fed tax	State tax	Net pay
4	1	Mary	$6	44				
5	2	Tom	$7	30				
6	3	Peter	$10	18				
7				Totals				

Fig. 2. Screenshots of starter templates for company profit modeling (adopted from Hoag, 2008; p. 245)

Being aware that subject matter and technological prerequisites influence the results of modeling, Kadijevich (2012) examined spreadsheet errors and reasons for them for simple deterministic spreadsheet models. These models, which analyzed the profitability of some businesses, in terms of four basic arithmetic operations, were built by first-year undergraduate business students within a course on business informatics. These students had to choose business situations themselves, analyze these situations, and give recommendations (based upon appropriate 'what-if' analyses) that make them profitable or more profitable. Instead of providing some starter templates, the course instructor (the author of this chapter) explained to the students a simple model of a taxi service (see Figure1 on p. 23) and the use of **Goal Seek** command to arrive at a proper recommendation. A detailed analysis of the students' models revealed equally frequent errors in selecting variables, initializing variables, and relating variables. [These labels for quantitative errors seemed conceptually stronger than those used in Teo & Tan (1999).] It was found that these errors were not influenced by mathematical reasons (i.e., simple business mathematics required by models developed) or software complexity (i.e., using variables as cells that referred to other cells). These errors were also not influenced by the taxi service model, which explained all calculations required by models developed by students. They were primarily generated by the lack of knowledge concerning business situations being modeled with respect to fixed and variable costs involved as well as proper values of some input variables. Having in mind that problem structuring and articulation is a central activity in design tasks (Jonassen, 2000), the three spreadsheet errors stemmed not only from a poor or incomplete knowledge of the business under scrutiny, but also from poor skills in problem structuring and integrating its parts with respect to costs, incomes, and profits.

Implications for spreadsheet learning

Spreadsheet learning should help learners recognize spreadsheet errors and reduce them. Bearing in mind the content of the two previous sections, this learning should take care about: (1) quantitative and qualitative spreadsheet errors, (2) sources of these errors, and (3) problem structuring in spreadsheet development.

As said previously, spreadsheet errors can be of two kinds: quantitative that can (and frequently do) change bottom-line values, and qualitative that do not change these values but deteriorate spreadsheet design. Quantitative errors may be categorized as omission, mechanical, and logic errors. Another categorization makes a distinction among errors in selecting variables, initializing variables, and relating variables. Because, apart from basic calculations, spreadsheet models may also use simulations or optimizations, quantitative errors may, in general, be examined as errors in selecting, initializing, and relating modeling objects. These modeling ob-

28

jects can be variables, distributions (in simulations), or relations (in optimizations). Regarding qualitative errors, as already underlined, spreadsheet developers may use formulas that contain numbers (jamming errors) and have the same datum or data at two or more places (duplication errors). The first qualitative error should, in general, be viewed as an instance of using modeling objects that contain numbers, a conceptually easier yet error-prone practice that should be avoided. [In modeling simulations with the normal distribution, the developer may, for example, use =NORMINV(RAND(), 1000, 100), but a better solution is to replace 1000 and 100 with the addresses of cells that contain the values of the mean and standard deviation (1000 and 100 in this example, and these may change). In modeling optimizations, a relation like $3 * D5 + 4 * E5 < 300$ should be replaced by a less error-prone, yet conceptually harder relation $C3 * D5 + C4 * E5 < F5$, where cells C3, C4, and F5 respectively contain numbers 3, 4, and 300 (which may be changed).] The second qualitative error may particularly be error-prone when it is an instance of duplication and jamming error (e.g., the value of tax rate is given in cell C5 and in a formula in cell D10). Of course, instead of a constant, a duplication error may refer to a formula repeated.

Regarding sources of spreadsheet errors, learners should be aware of different competencies involved in spreadsheet modeling and improve some of them if needed. These competencies deal with the knowledge of: (a) the business situation being modeled, (b) the business mathematics applicable to this situation, (c) the informatics (computer science) concepts that may be used to make this mathematics alive, and (d) the software applied (i.e., its affordances, interface, and built-in behavior). Knowledge under (d) may, for example, be improved through examining unusual or borderline uses of spreadsheet functions or other affordances, such as the application of a function with both expected and unexpected data types. It can also be done through exploring the limits in error detection by the software. For example, the auto-correction feature may add a forgotten parenthesis at the end of a formula, but this may be wrong as it must be added somewhere inside the formula. (See Tort, 2010, for this approach.)

Knowledge under (a)–(c) may be improved through the activity of problem structuring, which is, as already underlined, a central activity in design tasks. Furthermore, problem structuring should take priority over problem solving (Dunn's view cited in Veselý, 2007). Problem structuring in our business context may comprise three interdependent phases: problem definition, problem specification, and problem sensing (adopted from

Dunn's framework presented in *ibid*). We start from a business situation and transform it into a business problem by using problem definition, which, for example, addresses what to examine, in which terms, and to what extent. Then we transform this business problem into a formal problem through problem specification, which may primarily address what input and output variables to use, which model to apply, what computations to define, which distributions to use, what relations to define, and what checks to apply. Finally, through the phase of problem sensing that critically looks at activities in the previous two phases, we examine whether and if so, to what extent this formal problem corresponds to the original business situation. Although the designer may focus on the phase of problem specification whereby he/she develops a techno-mathematical representation of the business problem, an improvement of knowledge under (a)–(c) requires a reflective practice of all three phases, addressing the above-mentioned and other relevant issues.

Implications for teacher education

In order to support better spreadsheet learning, this education should examine spreadsheet errors. These errors may be examined in a general sense, like in the case of above-mentioned quantitative errors in selecting, initializing, and relating modeling objects (variables in simple deterministic models, distributions in simulations, or equations and inequalities in optimizations). Teacher education also should examine sources of these errors (business situation being modeled, business mathematics applicable to this situation, informatics concepts that may be used to make this mathematics alive, and the software applied), and strengthen and connect these sources through various activities involving, for example, problem structuring and a usual software exploration mentioned on the previous page.

Apart from clarifying mathematical and computer science concepts related to spreadsheet modeling and the acquisition of solid knowledge of the spreadsheet tool used (i.e. its affordances, interface, and built-in behavior), there is a great need to support the learning of basic features of some spreadsheet auditing tools (including main underlying concepts), whereby the quality of data, model, and its elements (e.g., formulas, distributions, relations) can be improved. Although building complex and error-free spreadsheet models is not attainable, the use of auditing tools and various developer-defined checks would improve matters.

In order to support better spreadsheet practice, teacher education

30

should promote a good spreadsheet design. As already underlined, this design calls for the use of: (a) separate areas for input data, intermediate results, output data, and check data, (b) formulas that do not contain numbers, (c) formulas in a row or a column that have the same structure, and (d) several formulas instead of one complex formula.

Bearing in mind the positive educational effects of using short videos in several subjects (Galbraith & Stillman, 2006; Bennedsen & Caspersen, 2008; Harraway, 2012), better spreadsheet learning may be promoted by presenting good spreadsheet practice in that way. Short videos may also be used for other issues discussed in this final part (e.g., basic computer science concepts materialized in spreadsheets). These videos may, for example, be based upon principles suggested by Clark and Mayer (2011). In addition, they may be realized in the tradition of minimalism. This is, in short, an approach to the design of document and instruction that calls for solving tasks that are personally meaningful and motivating in direct, solver-tailored ways with the smallest amount of the instructional verbiage (Carroll, 1998).

As already underlined, studies on spreadsheet learning and teaching have been missing in research in computer science education despite the fact that competent work with spreadsheets is required at most workplaces. In order to support a better spreadsheet learning and practice, this research may focus on several areas including (1) spreadsheet errors and sources of them, (2) critical issues of spreadsheet design, and (3) difficulties in spreadsheet auditing. In doing so, researchers may use, as done in research presented in this chapter, an integrated approach that considers and combines different perspectives of the subject, taking into account relevant findings from related areas such as management, modeling, and programming.

Acknowledgement. This contribution is dedicated to the author's son Aleksandar. It resulted from the author's work on projects OI-174012 and III-44006 funded by the Serbian Ministry of Education, Science and Technological Development. The author expresses his gratitude to Esther Polenezer for the proofreading of this chapter and Branimir Trošić for help in the preparation of this book for publication.

References

Bennedsen, J., & Caspersen, M. E. (2008). Exposing the programming process. In J. Bennedsen, M. E. Caspersen & M. Kölling (Eds.), Reflections on the teaching of programming. *Lecture Notes in Computer Science*, Vol. 4821, pp. 6–16. Berlin: Springer.

Carroll, J. M. (Ed.) (1998). *Minimalism beyond the Nurnberg funnel*. Cambridge, MA: The MIT Press.

Clark, R. C., & Mayer, R. E. (2011). *E-learning and the science of instruction: Proven guidelines for consumers and designers of multimedia learning* (3rd ed.). San Francisco, CA: Pfeiffer.

Croll, G. J. (2005). The importance and criticality of spreadsheets in the city of London. In D. Ward (Ed.), *Proceedings of the EuSpRIG 2005 conference: Managing spreadsheets in the light of Sarbanes-Oxley* (pp. 82–92). London: EuSpRIG. Retrieved December 4, 2012, from http://arxiv.org/abs/0709.4063v2

Croll, G. J. (2009). Spreadsheets and the financial collapse. In D. Ward & G. Croll (Eds.), *Proceedings of the EuSpRIG 2009 conference: The role of spreadsheets in organisational excellence* (pp. 145–161). London: EuSpRIG. Retrieved December 4, 2012, from http://arxiv.org/abs/0908.4420v1

Galbraith P., & Stillman G. (2006). A framework for identifying student blockages during transitions in the modeling process. *Zentralblatt für Didaktik der Mathematik, 38*(2), 143–162.

Harraway, J. A. (2012). Learning statistics using motivational videos, real data and free software. *Technology Innovations in Statistics Education, 6*(1). Retrieved December 4, 2012, from http://escholarship.org/uc/uclastat_cts_tise

Hesse, R., & Scerno, D. H. (2009). How electronic spreadsheets changed the world. *Interfaces, 42*(2), 159–167.

Hoag, J. A. (2008). College student novice spreadsheet reasoning and errors (doctoral dissertation). Corvallis, OR: Oregon State University. Retrieved December 4, 2012, from http://ir.library.oregonstate.edu/xmlui/bitstream/handle/1957/9324/Hoag%20dissertation.pdf

Hoyles, C., Noss, R., Kent, P., & Bakker, A. (2010). *Improving mathematics at work: The need for techno-mathematical literacies.* London: Routledge.

Jonassen D. H. (2000). Toward a design theory of problem solving. *Educational Technology Research and Development, 48*(4), 63–85.

Kadijevich, Dj. (2010). Using spreadsheets in the finance industry. In A. Araújo, A. Fernandes, A. Azevedo & J. F. Rodrigues (Eds.), *Proceedings of the EIMI 2010 conference: Educational interfaces between mathematics and industry* (pp. 311–320). Coimbra, Portugal: Centro Internacional de Matemática.

Kadijevich, Dj. (2012). Examining errors in simple spreadsheet modeling from different research perspectives. *Journal of Educational Computing Research, 47*(2),137–153.

Kulesz, D. (2011). From good practices to effective policies for preventing errors in spreadsheets. In S. Thorne & G. Croll (Eds.), *Proceedings of the EuSpRIG 2011 conference: Spreadsheet governance – Policy and practice* (pp. 61–72). London: EuSpRIG. Retrieved December 4, 2012, from http://arxiv.org/abs/1111.6878v1

O'Beirne P. (2008). Information and data quality in spreadsheets. In D. Ward (Ed.), *Proceedings of the EuSpRIG 2008 conference: In pursuit of spreadsheet excellence* (pp. 171–185). London: EuSpRIG. Retrieved December 4, 2012, from http://arxiv.org/abs/0809.3609

O'Beirne P. (2009). Checks and controls in spreadsheets. In D. Ward & G. Croll (Eds.), *Proceedings of the EuSpRIG 2009 conference: The role of spreadsheets in organisational excellence* (pp. 1–7). London: EuSpRIG. Retrieved December 4, 2012, from http://arxiv.org/abs/0908.1186v1

Powell S. G., Baker K. R., & Lawson B. (2008). A critical review of the literature on spreadsheet errors. *Decision Support Systems, 46*(1), 128–138.

Powell S. G., Baker K. R., & Lawson, B. (2009a). Errors in operational spreadsheets. *Journal of Organizational and End User Computing, 1*(3), 4–36.

Powell S. G., Baker K. R., & Lawson B. (2009b). Impact of errors in operational spreadsheets. *Decision Support Systems, 47*(2), 126–132.

Spreadsheet management: Not what you figured (2009). Deloitte. Retrieved December 4, 2012, from www.deloitte.com/assets/Dcom-UnitedStates/Local%20Assets/Documents/AERS/us_risk_spreadsheet_mgt_022509%20(2).pdf

Learning about spreadsheets

Spreadsheet mistakes (2009, December). PricewaterhouseCoopers Cyprus. Retrieved December 4, 2012, from
www.pwc.com.cy/en_CY/cy/challenges/assets/pwc-cy-spreadsheet-mistakes-2.pdf

Steen L. A. (2003). Data, shapes, symbols: Achieving balance in school mathematics. In B. L. Madison & L. A. Steen (Eds.), *Quantitative literacy: Why numeracy matters for schools and colleges* (pp. 53–74). Princeton, NJ: National Council on Education and the Disciplines.

Teo T. S. H., & Tan M. (1999). Spreadsheet development and 'what-if' analysis: quantitative versus qualitative errors. *Accounting, Management & Information Technologies*, *9*(3), 141–160.

Tort F. (2010). Spreadsheet teaching: Principles to design a curriculum. In S. Thorne (Ed.), *Proceedings of the EuSpRIG 2010 conference*: *Practical steps to protect organisations from out-of-control spreadsheets* (pp. 99–110). London: EuSpRIG. Retrieved December 4, 2012, from http://arxiv.org/abs/1009.2787

Tort, F., Blondel, F.-M., & Bruillard, É. (2008). Spreadsheet knowledge and skills of French secondary school students. In R. T. Mittermeir & M. M. Sysło (Eds.), ISSEP 2008. *Lecture Notes in Computer Science*, Vol. 5090, pp. 305–316. Berlin: Springer.

The state of data quality today (2009, July). An information difference research study. Retrieved December 4, 2012, from www.pbsoftware.eu/uk/files/download/analyst-reports/TheStateofDataQualityTodaybyInformationDifference.pdf

Veselý, A. (2007). Problem delimitation in public policy analysis. *Central European Journal of Public Policy*, *1*(1), 80–100. Retrieved December 4, 2012, from www.cejpp.eu

3

PERSONALIZING LEARNING ABOUT DATABASES

Peter K. Antonitsch

Learning, structuring, and individualization go together. Learning aims at mastering the structures that surround us and denotes the creation of corresponding internal structures: John D. Nolan points at the necessity to chunk and categorize in order to master new information (Nolan, 1973), while Jerome Bruner states that "unless detail is placed into a structured pattern, it is rapidly forgotten" (Bruner, 2003, p. 24). These findings of pedagogy are supported by neurobiological research. External structures we recognize and remember are represented in our brains by neuronal patterns that are generated by the brain itself due to repetitive stimuli. (Spitzer, 2003, pp. 79). Consequently, creating internal structures (or: learning) depends on the learning individual.

Teaching and learning: A survey of relevant structures

In school, learning means to become acquainted with mindsets and specific structures of various subject matters. While many of these structures seem to be artificial at first, they have been found appropriate to model certain aspects of the surrounding environment. Hence, teaching means to reveal the structure of a certain topic and to support the construction of corresponding internal structures by means of learning activities that allow learners to apply their newly established knowledge or skills. Teachers have to know the basic structures of the content that is being taught. Furthermore, teachers have to be aware of structures that guide individual learning processes. Based upon knowledge about relevant structures, it is the teacher's task to provide a framework for the learners to structure their own learning processes. These three levels of structures have to be considered when aiming at personalization of learning processes and deserve closer examination.

The structure of learning content

Thinking about the structure of learning content has to deal with a certain topic. The author chooses the topic databases of the subject matter to point at the dual structure inherent in learning content.

When learning Informatics, learners are expected to apply control- and data-structures to create programs that provide a (dynamic) solution for a given problem. Contrary to that, when working with tools like databases, learners use structures to describe and/or investigate a certain (static) aspect of the world. Consequently, knowing about and working with structures has to be considered a key issue in informatics education.

But informatics education has to serve two different goals. On the one hand, the subject matter informatics deals with what is called informatics proper, focusing on "Fundamental Ideas of Computer Science" (Schwill, 1994) or "Great Principles in Computing" (Denning, 2003) and emphasizing (conceptual) knowledge about information and about the organization of hard- and software. This aspect of structuring has been described above. On the other hand, the subject matter informatics has to deliver skills (or: procedural knowledge) enabling one to use application software like text processors or spreadsheet programs. This part of informatics education is commonly referred to as "Information and Communication Technology" (short: ICT), and focuses on the structure of software tools.

While most of the topics in Informatics education are considered either part of ICT or informatics (proper), databases belong to both. Databases have become common tools to store, sort, and retrieve data from various fields of knowledge, for instance, when being used as "mindtools" (in the meaning of: tools to think with) to organize content (Jonassen, 2006). Using databases this way mainly requires procedural knowledge to master the structure of the database software and to conceptualize the representation of data in tables. In addition, techniques to design and implement databases are part of database education, as well. These topics stress the structure of the underlying relational representation of data and call for modeling and abstraction. Modeling and abstraction are considered basic concepts of informatics proper and represent the second dimension of database-structure Informatics education has to deal with.

Corresponding to these two levels of database structures, two different instructional patterns have evolved that guide the teaching of databases. The application-oriented approach to the structure of database software is being addressed by certificate-based user training like the European Computer Driving License, ECDL (2008) and follows an instructional pattern that has been named practising skills (Antonitsch, 2006). This pattern provides examples of (in most cases flat-file) databases and focuses on entering, storing, retrieving and presenting data. Therefore, special attention is directed toward forms for data input or reporting tools, while the database core is neglected. The second instructional pattern has been labeled providing insight (Antonitsch, 2006) and emphasizes the underlying relational structure of data. Being inspired by database curricula at university level, this pattern follows the steps of conceptual database design, logical database design, data entry, and exploiting the database structure by means of database queries.

By providing two different instructional patterns, database education points at knowledge about the structure of the learning content and at skills to apply this structural knowledge as different aspects of content structure. Both of these complementary aspects have to be regarded when designing learning activities, and, at its best, both of them should be combined within a single pedagogical pattern.

Cognitive structures in content learning

Choosing which structures to teach is a prerequisite for teaching, but choosing how to present these structures to stimulate transfer into internal structures on the side of the learners is yet another prerequisite. Quite often teachers become aware that learning tasks, although deliberately chosen, miss the audience.

Researchers in cognitive mathematics discovered two different cognitive structures that guide the transfer of external structures into an internal representation. According to I. Schwank we have to "distinguish between a predicative structure, which is more concentrated on networks of relations and structures, and a functional structure, which lays preference on thinking in terms of effects and on organizing sequences of actions" (Schwank, 1993). Involuntarily, people employ one of these cognitive structures or the other. In doing so, they develop different perspectives for a given situation/problem and use different strategies to comprehend its structure. Consequently, learning is at its best when the external representation of a situation/problem meets the preferred cognitive structure of the learner.

Learners who prefer a predicative point of view can be expected to underachieve, if learning tasks are presented in a functional way and vice versa. Therefore, to do justice to both types of cognitive structures, the structure of the learning content should be presented in both ways. Modern click'n code programming environments like Scratch or NXT-G give an idea of how to achieve this: Instead of textual coding, program instructions are represented by graphic icons that can be combined into runnable programs. These "programming bricks" are static elements that can form a structure providing a certain functionality (Antonitsch, 2009). While the former supports a predicative approach to programming structures, the latter promotes the functional point of view considering the dynamics of a running program.

Structuring through competence-oriented learning

To decide upon the learning content and the way to present its structure is the teacher's share in structuring the learning process. But teachers can be catalysts, at the most: Construction of internal structures demands active participation of the learners, who have to take responsibility for their own learning process.

This guiding idea of self-organized learning has attracted broader attention in the face of competence-oriented education, corresponding to upcoming competence-based curricula that resemble outcomes-based education. This is "an approach to planning, delivering and evaluating instruction that requires [...] teachers and students to focus their attention and efforts on the desired results of education" (Killen, 2000). Competence-orientation supplements competence-based curricula with personalized/individualized learning: Learners should be enabled to follow an individual learning path, thus transforming predefined common and compulsory learning goals into individual learning goals (Müller, 2003).

With competence-orientation, learners need information about the learning objectives, about ways to reach their goals and about means to test whether they have succeeded or not, or rather: to what extent they have succeeded to reach the goals. To provide this information, a competence matrix (or: rubric) is the tool of choice: A competence matrix pairs rows with learning goals and columns with different levels of competence-acquisition where each cell contains a description of what one must do to prove that (level of) competence (see Table 1 overleaf).

As each learner should be enabled to acquire a specific competence according to his or her abilities, the competence matrix indicates what the learner must be able to do in order to prove the acquisition of a certain level of competence. Additionally, a competence matrix can be used by the learner to mark the levels of the listed competences he or she has already reached. This yields an individual competence profile helping to decide on further learning steps to improve the learner's competences. Furthermore, competence matrices should be accompanied by checklists of learning tasks, which list tasks designed to acquire a certain competence at a desired level. Learners turn to active learners when using competence matrices and checklists to choose tasks appropriate to reach a certain level of competence and according to the learners' individual abilities. Moreover these tools can be used by the learners to prove the success of their learning processes.

	A1	A2	B1
Theory and Basic Handling	I can name the most important parts of a computer.	I know about the principles of computers like data storage or random access memory. I know about areas of application for computers.	I can name the parts of a PC. I can distinguish internal devices (like display boards) from peripherals (like USB sticks). I can relate the most important abbreviations and names to the corresponding devices.
Computer Usage and Data Management	I can start and run programs, store and print data. I can shut down the operating system properly.	I can open files that I have stored on a network drive or a USB-stick, modify them and store them in various ways using the „save as" option.	I can use the tools provided by the desktop environment in a competent way: I can manage files and folders (rename, delete, copy, move, etc.) I know how to use desktop-icons and screen-windows. I know how to search for specific files.

Tab. 1. Competence-matrix (snippet) for the subject matter informatics;
source: www.institut-beatenberg.ch/images/pdf/kompetenzraster/kompetenzraster.pdf
(in German, translated by the author)

A proposal to combine different levels of structure

The tools of competence-oriented education add a structural framework supporting a personalized approach to the structures to be learned (and taught). Hence competence orientation and personalization call for combining the levels of structure described in the first part. On the side of the teachers, this denotes a shift from traditional instruction to coaching of personalized learning processes. Generally speaking, instructional patterns have to be replaced by learning patterns that give learning prominence over teaching by providing an appropriate learning environment and a corresponding methodical framework. Returning to the structure of database-content this section first of all addresses the following questions:

• Is there a way to combine the two instructional patterns of database education identified in the first section into a single learning pattern promoting procedural and conceptual knowledge?

• How should a learning environment look so that learners can turn from passive consumers of knowledge into active creators of competence in the field of (database) structures? And:

• What methodical issues have to be considered by teachers so that learners not only learn how to apply ready-to-use rules within the structure of databases (and database-software) and know about the structure, but also understand the structure?

First answers have been given a few years ago when the author developed a first proposal for a learning pattern in database education (Antonitsch, 2006 or 2007). In the following, this pattern shall be outlined and augmented by considering cognitive structures and competence orientation.

Forming an appropriate database learning environment

The two instructional patterns, practicing skills and providing insight, are coupled by the tabular structure of relational databases and overlap at database queries (Antonitsch, 2006). An interface of that kind is a necessary condition to combine two different instructional patterns complementing each other. Consequently, the proposed learning pattern builds on database queries. In doing so it considers both procedural and conceptual knowledge in the following ways:

Learners are guided to plan queries in order to understand the relational structure of databases. In turn, learners have to use this conceptual knowledge about the relational structure to conduct queries or, in other words, to apply procedural knowledge about database software. Database queries provide (new) information about the modeled system. This information can be related to the database model and helps to improve conceptual knowledge about modeling. Finally, learners have to apply this knowledge by creating database structures by themselves, which, again, aims at deepening conceptual knowledge. This process to learn about structures by investigating a given structure and to use this knowledge to create similar but new structures has been called complete structuring (Antonitsch, 2006, 2007).

The proposed learning pattern builds upon a learning environment that is based on a ready-to-use database. A database model of some aspect of school life has proven to be a good choice: Learners should be well acquainted with the modeled system so that they can recognize familiar structures within the database model, explore the database model by themselves, and relate results of database queries to the real-world situation. Of course, the example database must not contain real data, and it must be of a certain size to allow for meaningful queries and, at the same time, of reduced complexity to foster the learners' individual exploration of the database structure. These contradicting requirements have been met by:

- Modeling each association as a table of its own so that every single piece of information has a tabular representation of its own.
- Restricting the database model to simple associations but avoiding aggregations and generalizations.
- Using a naming pattern that helps to distinguish between tables that represent associations from tables that represent entities.

Furthermore, the learning environment makes extensive use of visualizing aids like relationship diagrams that represent the overall structure of a database (Figure 1), or different views upon the structure of a single table (Figure 2).

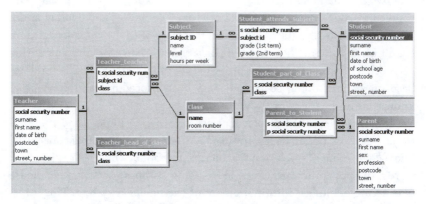

Fig. 1 Relationship diagram representing the structure of the proposed example database

This learning environment has been found to support the learners when dealing with database structures and provides an answer to the second question posed above. Furthermore, by combining aspects of conceptual and procedural knowledge, it addresses the first question, too. But to form a learning pattern, the learning environment needs to be complemented by a methodical framework that guides the learners to explore the basic database structures mainly by themselves. Here, to guide means to pose questions about relevant structures, to offer tasks that trigger active exploration and to point at available tools that can support the exploration process. These guiding ideas will be exemplified below by sketching the intended course of database exploration.

General methodical considerations ...

The initial phase of the learning process aims at understanding the basic structure. In the case of relational databases, the first step is to learn what databases are for, to learn some basic vocabulary like association or attribute, and to learn how to read relationship diagrams. Within the learning environment the learners can be guided by questions like: "What do rectangles and connecting lines in the relationship diagram represent?" or: "What is the difference between attributes printed in bold face and those printed with normal font?" to discover – in the words of learners – "identifying attributes" and "connecting attributes." Notably, terms like these should be used for a while as they make more sense to the learners than the terminus primary key used in scientific debate.

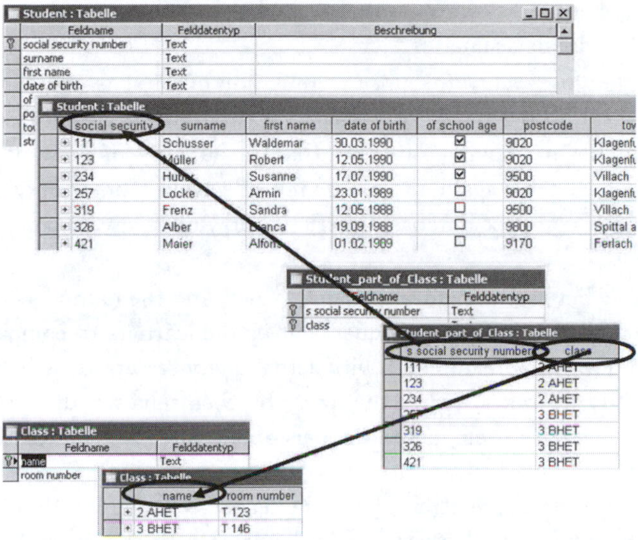

Fig. 2. Comprehending the table-structure of databases and the connection between tables by means of different views onto tables provided by database software

Next, the learners' attention switches from the macro-structure of the database to the structure of single tables. Contrasting the designer view onto database tables with the data stored within a table shows that all the rectangles of the relationship diagram are tables. This can be used to clarify how connecting attributes are used to relate two tables by drawing connection diagrams like the one shown in Figure 2. Having learners draw further examples of detailed connection diagrams has been found to be a good introductory exercise in database design.

The last step of the initial phase prepares the learners for database queries by means of navigation tasks like: "You want to know the names of all the teachers who teach the class of student Joe Miller. Use the connecting lines of the relationship diagram to find all the tables that are needed to obtain that information." Once again the learners are directed to examine the macro-structure of the database by looking for a connecting path between information scattered all over the database.

Having learned about the structure of relational data representation and how to read its graphical representations, the learners are expected to apply their conceptual knowledge. They start to query the example database using a query designer. From a structural point of view, this graphical tool has various advantages, just to name a few:

- Query designers create database queries based on information about tables containing the information and connections between them. Therefore, learners can reuse their knowledge about connecting paths to formulate database queries.

- Query designers allow for quick formulation of database queries. Hence learners can gain a lot of experience with database queries in comparably short time. Once having found out that the outcome of a database query is a database table again and can be reused within a new query, learners can create complex database queries following a divide and conquer strategy.

- Switching between the query designer's view and the data view provided by the table resulting from a query allows the learners to compare their expectations for the outcome with actual query results. This helps them to identify mistakes within the query by themselves and, at the same time, to validate their mental models about the structure of the database.

Querying the database strengthens the learner's understanding of database structures and prepares for the last phase of the learning process where the learners have to apply their knowledge about structures to create new structures when designing databases by themselves.

... and the importance of good tasks

Active learning relies on good tasks that motivate learners to start their individual learning processes. Thus, besides an appropriate learning environment and didactical intentions coupled with general methodical considerations, good tasks form the third constituent of a learning pattern. Of course, good tasks within the proposed database learning pattern deal with questions that have to be answered by means of database queries. Some examples for good tasks are the following (Antonitsch, 2006):

- The answer to the question "Do students whose parents are teachers get better marks in school?" necessitates collecting information about students whose parents are teachers and about those whose parents have a different profession. The learners have to use the structure provided by the database example, extend it by creating new tables from database queries, and compare the data contained within the new tables.

Furthermore, learners have been found to respond to the outcome of this query, no matter whether the used data set indicates that teachers' children get better marks or not. Learners simply started discussing the situation at their school and how the school modeled by the example database corresponds to their own school reality. Besides deepening the learners' understanding of database structures this task promotes reflecting about structures, both of which make it a good task in the above sense.

- Open-ended tasks like "Do students whose parents are teachers have greater success in school?" or rather provocative questions like: "Which teachers are absent from school most of the time?" are further examples for good tasks within the database learning pattern. While the first question lets the learners think about the meaning of success before they can start to formulate the corresponding query, the learners find that the second question simply cannot be answered with the data provided by the database and makes learners think about the quality of the example database.

Of course, the second question from above was not at all chosen by accident: Questions that cannot be answered within the database can point out structural shortcomings to the learners. For instance, modeling every association as a table of itself makes it impossible to represent so called "one to one" or "one to n" associations in the provided example database: The table "Teacher_head_of_class" can associate the name of a teacher with several classes or, reversely, one class with the names of several teachers, while in most schools strictly one teacher is supposed to be head of one class. In the best case, learners start thinking about different ways to represent associations by themselves. In any case, problem-awareness opens the learner's minds to the solution proposed by the teacher.

How to deal with the structure of content?

The described course of actions, good tasks, and the learning environment form a structuring loop. Starting off with learning about database structures that are not perfect on purpose, the learners prepare themselves to apply their knowledge to database queries. In turn, results of database queries point at limitations of the structures in use. Judging from experience, this leads not only to learning but also to understanding of principles of database structures and to reflecting about the structure of the modeled system.

Furthermore, it turns out that, within a learning pattern, the learning environment and methodical considerations that become visible within good tasks depend on each other. Hence the questions posed at the beginning of this section cannot be answered separately.

The structure of the learning content has to be the starting point for designing a learning pattern. Most likely, the learning content covers different levels of structure that can be related to conceptual or procedural knowledge, respectively. In that case an interface between these different levels of content structure should be the core of an appropriate learning environment. The learning environment constitutes an important component of the learning pattern.

Models that represent relevant structures within the learning environment should be big enough to allow for meaningful exploration. For instance, databases within the database learning environment should consist of at least eight to ten tables. Smaller databases, on the one hand, might provide only a subset of typical database structures. On the other hand, data contained within only a few tables do not require the use of a database management system and can be managed with spreadsheet software much easier. Of course, example databases of that size have to be provided by the teacher and of course models of certain complexity have to use some kind of visualization.

Furthermore, the models provided for the learners' exploration should refer to an aspect of the real world the learners are familiar with. This makes it much easier to find tasks that make sense within the learning environment and are meaningful to the learners. Tasks of that kind have been called good tasks. Good tasks are methodical tools to guide the learners' exploration processes and turn the learning environment into a learning pattern.

Finally, as has been argued above, a model that is imperfect but accompanied by good tasks pointing at the model's structural peculiarities has the potential to create cognitive conflicts in the learner's brain. Cognitive conflicts, in turn, are starting points of individual learning processes. Hence "a didactically well chosen database example usually is not a perfect example in the sense of a real-world representation but an example that triggers questioning and exploration" (Antonitsch, 2007).

Stepping beyond the structure of content

Up to this point all considerations deal with the structure of content. But, at a closer look, the described learning pattern takes account of both cognitive structures named in the first section as well. Although the learning environment relies upon the static representation of database structure, the formulation of good tasks allows for predicative and functional strategies of problem solving. Guided by the visualization of database structure, learners preferring a predicative approach can look for connecting paths by analyzing the pattern displayed by the relationship diagram. Learners who prefer a functional approach can explore the database structure by (mentally) moving along the connecting lines in the relationship diagram and process relations in order to collect information needed for a certain query. Furthermore, learners can explore the changes within the tables that result from database queries when the query is varied by adding or dropping certain restrictions. This adds another functional aspect to database queries. Judging from experience, the diversity of possible (cognitive) approaches fosters the exploration of database structure. Corresponding to their individually preferred cognitive structure, learners become active constructors of (structural) knowledge and understanding users of database software.

Nevertheless, having been developed before competence-orientation gained broader attention, the learning pattern falls short of regarding personalized learning in the sense outlined in the first section. Despite talking about a learning pattern, it is still the teacher who directs the course of the learning process. Current considerations aim at adding a framework for competence-oriented learning. In order to pass responsibility for their learning processes to the learners, the learning pattern has to be enriched by structuring aids like a competence matrix. Referring to experience from an attempt to introduce competence matrices, task sheets, and competence-oriented forms of assessment into programming courses at upper secondary level (Antonitsch, 2011), a proposal for a matrix that translates the intentions of the proposed learning pattern and corresponds to database issues in the new competence-oriented curriculum for Austrian vocational schools is given in Table 2.

Different from the example competence matrix in Table 1, the competence levels are labeled from D to A with D denoting the lowest level of a competence. Four levels have been chosen to correspond to positive grades in the Austrian grading scheme. Furthermore, the descriptions of competence levels are rather general and are accompanied by links to corresponding tasks that concretize the competences regarding the learning environment in use. This points at an important issue for the teaching practitioner: While a general competence matrix can be provided for a certain area of competences, such a template has to be adapted to meet the conditions of a certain setting provided for the learners: This concerns good tasks, a sufficient number of which should be provided for each level of competence to let the learners follow their individual learning paths. Good tasks within the learning pattern are coupled with example databases that describe an aspect of reality the learners are familiar with. Besides "school," modeling an online shop or a social network can be considered appropriate, but the number of proper examples seems to be limited. Furthermore, alternate forms of assessment have to be developed that support the monitoring of learning processes by the teacher and allow evaluating personalized learning progress. This issue has already been addressed in (Antonitsch, 2011) for programming courses, but has to be answered anew when dealing with different content in the face of competence orientation and personalization.

| Competence | Level of Competence | | | |
	D	C	B	A
0) I can use tools of a database management system at a basic level.	I can manage data stored in a database by means of database tables. → Tasks 0.1 to 0.4	I can manage data stored in a database by means of forms. → Tasks 0.5 to 0.8	I can select data stored in a database by applying filters. → Tasks 0.9 to 0.12	I can use reports to present selected data from a database. → Tasks 0.13 to 0.16
1) I can use tools of a database management system to obtain new information.	I can use the relationship diagram to find required data within a given database. → Tasks 1.1 to 1.4	I can use the relationship diagram and different views of tables to comprehend the structure of a given database. → Tasks 1.5 to 1.8	I can create QBE queries to obtain new information from a given database and to reflect upon the validity of the database model. → Task 1.9	I can create SQL queries to obtain new information from a given database and to reflect upon the validity of the database model. → Task 1.10
2) I can use a database management system to describe a certain aspect of the real world.	I can create simplified database-tables that describe a certain aspect of the real world. → Tasks 2.1 to 2.4	I can identify weaknesses of simplified database-tables in describing a certain aspect of the real world. → Tasks 2.5 to 2.8	I can design a conceptual model that provides a better description of a real-world aspect than simplified database-tables. → Tasks 2.9 to 2.12	I can transform a conceptual model into a corresponding structure of database-tables. → Tasks 2.13 to 2.16

Tab 2. A proposal for a competence matrix for database education

But does it pay off to combine the different levels of structure, to consider the structure of content, the cognitive structures of learning, and the structures that are needed to support personalized learning?

D. H. Jonassen points at conceptual change as "one of the most common conceptions of meaningful learning" and states: "Conceptual change occurs when learners change their understanding of the concepts they use and the conceptual frameworks that encompass them." Furthermore, he suggests databases as one of the tools that foster conceptual change when used to model domain knowledge, problems, or experiences (Jonassen, 2006). There, databases are seen solely as tools to model content and discover interrelations or similarities of the modeled content. The proposed learning pattern extends meaningful learning regarding databases. By combining several levels of structuring it includes personalized learning about and – by means of the structural loop mentioned above – understanding of the optimal structure to store and to relate raw data within a database. Understanding what has been a "black box" before has to be considered conceptual change. Furthermore, understanding of database structures supports applying databases as mind tools for conceptual change in other fields of knowledge as described by Jonassen. Combining different levels of structure and turning learners into active learners has added value compared with classical forms of teacher-centered instruction solely focusing on the structure of content.

Implications for teacher professional development

Multiple levels of structure are not unique to databases and database education or to secondary education. It was merely the existence of two different instructional patterns that turned the author's attention to databases, which in this way have become a kind of prototypical content for dealing with different aspects of structuring in a novel way but using well-tried tools. Whenever society (embodied in national curricula) urges teachers to care about "understanding" and "applying," to consider different learning types and/or to personalize learning, double structuring is in place, with any content, within any subject matter.

First evidence of positive effects on the outcome of learning processes due to combining different levels of structure into learning patterns for the subject matter informatics is provided by personal experience (Antonitsch 2006, 2007, 2011). For the teacher shifting from well-tried instructional patterns to learning patterns first of all means to rethink the importance of the learning environment. Concerning the subject matter of informatics, available software tools used in schools very often have to be tailored to the needs of the learners so that they meet at least some of the advantages of mini-languages or microworlds that have become important learning aids in the field of programming (Brusilovsky et al., 1997): Learning environments have to be small or to be of reduced complexity and they have to be visually appealing. Furthermore, the structure of the learning environment has to provide questions that can be addressed by good tasks triggering the learner's active explorations.

Learner's individual preconditions for learning form a second aspect that has to be considered with learning patterns aiming to develop active learning into personalized learning. Personalization covers areas like cognitive structures in the learner's brain, individual learning styles (Prashnig, 2006) or findings of neurodidactics (Sabitzer, 2011; Sabitzer & Antonitsch, 2012) and opens new fields of interest for most of the teachers who traditionally have been used to focusing on content when designing lessons for class. All of these are areas of current research, findings of which have to be included in teacher education and training colleges for experienced and pre-service teachers. Furthermore, personalized learning calls for coaching and monitoring the individual learning processes. Although human teachers can be accompanied and supported by intelligent tutoring systems like Active Math (Melis, Haywood, & Smith, 2006), which are designed to respond to individual knowledge and needs of the learners, additional in-service training regarding corresponding soft skills seems to be necessary. Finally, personalization increases preparation work for teachers. Intensified cooperation among teachers, supposedly across the borders of established subject matters and team-teaching in class, can be considered a strategy to cope with this point.

References

Antonitsch, P. (2011). On competence-orientation and learning informatics. In D. Bezakova & I. Kalas (Eds.), *Informatics in schools: Situation, evolution and perspectives, Proceedings of ISSEP 2011, selected papers* (on a CD). Bratislava: Library and publishing centre, Comenius University.

Antonitsch P. (2009). From object-orientation to human-centredness. In J. Hromkovič, R. Královič, & J. Varenhold (Eds.), *ISSEP 2010 Proceedings of short communications* (pp. 1–15). Zürich: ETH Zürich.

Antonitsch P. (2007). Datenbanken – (etwas) anders gesehen. In S. Schubert (Ed.), Didaktik der Informatik in Theorie und Praxis, Proceedings of INFOS 2007 (pp. 229–240). *Lecture Notes in Informatics,* Vol. 112. Bonn: Gesellschaft für Informatik.

Antonitsch P. (2006). Databases as a tool of general education. In R. Mittermeir (Ed.), Informatics education – The bridge between using and understanding computers, Proceedings of ISSEP 2006 (pp. 59–70). *Lecture Notes in Computer Science,* Vol. 4226. Berlin: Springer.

Bruner J. (2003). *The process of education* (27th printing). Cambridge, MA & London: Harvard University Press.

Brusilovsky P., Calabrese E., Hvorecky J., Kouchnirenko A., & Miller P. (1997). Minilanguages: A way to learn programming principles. *Education and Information Technologies* 2(1), 65-83. Retrieved December 6, 2012, from www.sis.pitt.edu/~peterb/papers/minilang.html

Denning P. (2003). Great principles of computing. *Communications of the ACM,* 46(11), 15–20.

ECDL (2008). *ECDL core syllabus.* Retrieved December 6, 2012, from www.ecdl.at/core/downloads/ECDL_Core_Syllabus.pdf (in German).

Jonassen D. H. (2006). *Modeling with technology* (3rd ed.) Upper Saddle River: Pearson Education.

Killen R. (2000). *Outcomes-based education: Principles and possibilities.* Newcastle, Australia: University of Newcastle. Retrieved December 6, 2012, from http://drjj.uitm.edu.my/DRJJ/CONFERENCE/UPSI/OBEKillen.pdf

Melis E., Haywood J., & Smith T. J. (2006). LeActiveMath. In W. Nejdl & K. Tochtermann (Eds.), First European conference on technology enhanced learning, EC-TEL 2006 (pp. 660–666). *Lecture Notes in Computer Science,* Vol. 4227 Berlin: Springer.

Müller A. (2003). Dem Wissen auf der Spur. *Spirit of learning series.* Beatenberg: institut Beatenberg. Retrieved December 6, 2012 from www.institut-beatenberg.ch/images/publikationen-und-materialien/dossiers/dem_wissen_auf_der_spur.pdf (in German).

Personalizing learning about databases

Nolan J. D. (1973). Conceptual and rote learning in children. *Teachers College Record, 75*(2), 51–258.

Prashnig B. (2006). *Learning styles and personalized teaching*. New York: Continuum International Publishing Group.

Sabitzer B. (2011). Neurodidactics – A new stimulus in ICT and computer science education. In L. Gómez Chova, I. Candel Torres, & A. López Martìnez (Eds.), *INTED 2011 Proceedings CD* (pp. 5881–5889). Barcelona: International Association of Technology, Education and Development.

Sabitzer B., & Antonitsch P. (2012). Of bytes and brain? Informatics education meets neurodidactics. In L. Gómez Chova, I. Candel Torres, & A. López Martìnez, *INTED 2012 Proceedings CD* (pp. 2003–2012). Barcelona: International Association of Technology, Education and Development.

Schwank I. (1993). Cognitive structures and cognitive strategies in algorithmic thinking. In E. Lemut, B. du Boulay, & G. Dettori (Eds.), Cognitive models and intelligent environments for learning programming (pp 249–259). *NATO ASI Series F*, Vol. 111. Berlin: Springer.

Schwill A. (1994). Fundamental ideas of computer science. *EATCS-Bulletin*, 53, 274–295.

Spitzer M. (2003). *Lernen. Gehirnforschung und die Schule des Lebens*. Heidelberg, Berlin: Spektrum.

PART 2

METHODOLOGICAL PERSPECTIVES

VISUALIZATION OF PROGRAMMING

Mordechai Ben-Ari

Introduction

Software visualization

In an effort to improve the didactics of informatics in general and of programming in particular, educators have developed many pedagogical software tools, especially visual tools. The first attempt in 1981 was by Ronald Baecker who produced a file called Sorting Out Sorting that animated the execution of various sorting algorithms (Baecker, 1998). A comprehensive, though now somewhat dated, review of research on software visualization can be found in Stasko et al. (1998). Software visualization covers a wide range of topics as can be seen in the taxonomy given by Price, Baecker, and Small (1998). Most effort has been invested in at the abstract level of algorithm visualization (Hundhausen, Douglas, & Stasko, 2002; Shaffer et al., 2010). A website devoted to the topic contains links to hundreds of software tools (http://algoviz.org/). Our interest is at the more concrete level of program visualization.

Some of the earliest research on the visualization of programs was done within the framework of the logic programming language Prolog. In the 1980s, logic programming was considered to be much easier to learn than standard imperative programming because it is declarative. Instead of giving commands to computers, you simply declare the required relation between the input and the output, and the inference engine is responsible for finding a way of carrying out the computation. However, it turned out that a Prolog program is difficult to understand unless one understands how the inference engine works, so visualization software tools were developed to display the process of computation in Prolog. An important example was the Transparent Prolog Machine (Eisenstadt & Bray-shaw, 1988). As Prolog became less widely used, attention shifted to programming environments for imperative and object-oriented languages.

Programming environments

Initially, software developers worked with punched cards and then editors on character-based terminals. As technology developed, it became possible to develop software within Integrated Development Environments (IDEs) that fully exploited the graphical capabilities of modern workstations and personal computers. Currently, state-of-the-art IDEs like system Eclipse (http://eclipse.org/) and similar systems from software companies like Microsoft and Sun are highly sophisticated and use graphics to their fullest.

Since professional IDEs like Eclipse are far too complex and confusing for novices, software development environments that are friendly to novices have been developed. What all of these systems have in common is the use of a graphical user interface (GUI) together with syntax highlighting (displaying different colors for different constructs like keywords, variable names, and so on). Pedagogical IDEs range from the very elementary like DrJava (http://drjava.org/) to the very sophisticated like JGRASP (http://jgrasp.org/), which displays graphical control structure diagrams.

A breakthrough in pedagogical IDEs came with BlueJ (www.bluej.org), which enables students learning object-oriented programming to create objects and invoke methods interactively. (This facility has since been incorporated into JGRASP.) However, even an environment like BlueJ may not help when novices are faced with the difficulties of learning to program in an advanced programming language like Java (currently, the most popular language for teaching introductory programming, although others like Python are gaining ground). One of the problems of learning to program is that programming languages are static textual representations of the dynamic execution of a computation. Therefore, an obvious way of improving learning is to utilize graphical notations that are easier for many people to learn with. There are two main approaches: visual programming and visualization of programming.

Visual programming environments

Visual programming environments enable the learner to write programs using graphical notation. The notation is designed to prevent the learner from making syntax mistakes as in textual programming languages. This is very important because syntax mistakes can deflect learning from more fundamental concepts of computation. Furthermore, these environments enable the learner to write programs for animations such as simulations and games. The hope is that students will find these more motivating than standard data-processing problems like: "read a sequence of grades and compute their average."

One of the first visual programming environments was Agentsheets (Repenning & Sumner, 1995; www.agentsheets.com). It was later joined by academic projects, in particular, Alice (Dann, Cooper, & Pausch, 2009; http://alice.org/) and Scratch (Resnick et al., 2009; http://scratch.mit. edu/). (For a survey of programming environments for novices, see Kelleher & Pausch, 2005.) The main difference between Alice and Scratch is that the former can create sophisticated 3-dimensional animations, while the later is limited to simple 2-dimensional animations. We have chosen to work with Scratch because it is freely available and because we believe that the simple 2-dimensional animations would be sufficient to teach fundamental computer science concepts.

Program visualization

While visual programming environments are targeted at young people (although they are also used in universities as preparation for other courses), eventually, students of science, engineering, and other fields will have to learn to use "real" programming languages. This has proved to be a significant barrier to successful learning, so educators have developed software systems intended to facilitate learning at this level. Again, graphics are frequently seen as a way of improving learning. This article will focus on the Jeliot program animation system (Ben-Ari et al., 2011; www.cs.joensuu.fi/ jeliot/). A more recent development is that of program simulation as implemented for Python programs in UUhistle (Sorva & Sirkiä, 2010; www.uuhistle.org). The problem with program animation is that the student has a static role as an observer, while in program simulation the student works at a higher level of engagement by predicting the outcome of the execution steps of a program.

This chapter will report on our research and compare our experiences with two visual tools that we have investigated for use in teaching programming to novices: Scratch and Jeliot.

The Scratch visual programming environment

Scratch is a visual programming environment (see Figure 1). Students write programs by dragging-and-dropping blocks labeled with commands and operations; this totally prevents syntax errors. Scratch programs control the animation of sprites (images on a stage that have behavior associated with them in the form of scripts of blocks), thus providing a context that motivates students. The Scratch website holds millions of projects, many written by young students.

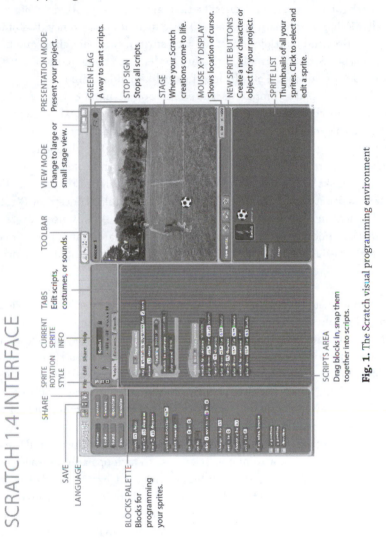

Fig. 1. The Scratch visual programming environment

Despite the flashy exterior of Scratch and the playful nature of the projects that most students develop, Scratch is really a highly sophisticated programming environment. The programming language supported by the blocks includes features seen in standard programming languages: numerical and string variables, the list which is similar to the widely used

ArrayList in Java and the standard control structures like if-statements and while-statements. It also supports graphical programming by controlling the animation of sprites on the stage; in addition, it supports drawing on the stage using a "pen" as in LOGO. Finally, it directly supports advanced software systems concepts that are only supported in libraries (called APIs) in standard languages. These include concurrency (both multiple sprites and multiple scripts for each sprite), event handling, and messages. Thus Scratch is an ideal medium for learning computer science: The concepts are advanced, but the interface is like a video game.

We developed a computer science textbook (Armoni & Ben-Ari, 2010) for middle-school students that was based upon incremental development of Scratch projects. That is, rather than the traditional organization of a programming textbook by topics (all about variables, all about control structures, etc.), each chapter was organized as a series of software development tasks in Scratch. Of course, we carefully designed the tasks so that their solution would require the use of the particular concept or Scratch construct that we wanted to teach. This textbook was used to teach Scratch in middle schools, and we carried out research intended to investigate the effectiveness of the intervention in learning computer science.

Research on learning with Scratch

The first question that we asked was what computer science knowledge the students actually learned (Meerbaum-Salant, Armoni, & Ben-Ari, 2010). This presented methodological problems. Whenever asking students a question or posing a problem to be solved, we had to understand what type and what level of knowledge we were demanding from them. Programming presents certain difficulties in categorizing problems and we had to develop a new categorization based upon a combination of the Revised Bloom Taxonomy and the SOLO taxonomy.

The results showed that in general students could successfully learn important concepts of computer science such as loops and message passing, although there were some problems with initialization, variables, and concurrency. We believe that the different levels of learning resulted from the correspondence or lack of it between concepts and constructs. Loops and message passing correspond to well-defined constructs in Scratch; for example, there is a construct broadcast [message] and a corresponding construct when I receive [message]. On the other hand, concepts like initialization do not correspond to particular constructs; instead, the concept refers to the use of any construct that sets a value such as a position or a direction, provided that the construct is used in a particular context – the beginning of a script. We believe that the solution to learning these advanced concepts lies in well-trained teachers who are thoroughly familiar with computer science concepts and who can bring students to understand the conceptual aspects of their programming.

The next part of our research arose serendipitously when we examined projects submitted to the yearly event Scratch Day organized by the developers of Scratch (http://wiki.scratch.mit.edu/wiki/Scratch_Day). We chose to solicit student projects and then to present prizes to the best ones, which were then demonstrated to all participants. We found that while students were capable of creating highly complex projects in Scratch, the quality of their programs, as evaluated according to the usual criteria for good software, left much to be desired (Meerbaum-Salant, Armoni, & Ben-Ari, 2011).

We can characterize the students' work as bricolage (Ben-Ari & Yeshno, 2006): a haphazard construction of a program by trial-and-error with no planning and no design. We called the strangest occurrence of this extreme bottom-up programming, where students dragged blocks for many commands and then tried to construct a program, frequently leaving unused commands in the script window. More serious was extremely fine-grained programming, where students used many small program fragments instead of combining them logically. Here is one example translated from the Scratch graphical blocks into text. To move a sprite until it touches another one, a simple conditional loop can be used:

```
repeat until <touching [target]>
    move (2) steps
```

Instead, one student used three different scripts each with a separate loop or condition:

```
forever
    move (2) steps
forever if <touching [target]>
    broadcast [stop]
when I receive [stop]
    stop all
```

This program lacks the cohesion and coherency that are central to good software. We called these bad habits of programming. Of course, one could argue that this is simply a different design that can be justified by the student who wrote it. That may be true, but we argue that the student did not design the software and that this structure just emerged; furthermore, we do not think – although this needs to be confirmed in further research – that the student could justify this design. Again, we believe that the solution lies with qualified teachers who demand that their students design their programs and be able to justify the design. We do not expect students to be able to use software engineering methodologies, notations, and tools, but we do think that in the case of Scratch they should be able to write a list of the sprites in the program and their scripts, and to be able to explain what each one does.

Visualization of programming

Program animation in Jeliot

The Jeliot program animation system (Ben-Ari et al., 2011; http://cs.joen-suu.fi/jeliot/) is a collaborative project between the Weizmann Institute of Science and the University of Joensuu (now part of the University of Eastern Finland). Jeliot is intended for novice learners of programming. It automatically generates detailed animations of textual programs written in the Java programming language (see Figure 2).

On the surface, it seems that Jeliot doesn't do much more than can be done with presentation software like PowerPoint or animation software like Flash. However, we cannot overemphasize the advantages of automatic generation of an animation. To prepare graphics using generic software requires a very large amount of time that educators simply do not have. Nor do most of them have the technical facility needed to use software such as Flash or the funding to hire an expert. Jeliot requires no more effort than writing an example program, something that an educator would do anyway when preparing for a lecture. Even better, a Jeliot animation can be created "of-the-fly" in response to a student's question, a capability that is totally beyond the range of generic software.

A further advantage of Jeliot is that it "understands" the program. The automatic generation of the animation requires Jeliot to parse the source program, so it knows technical details concerning variables, methods, types, and so on. This can be seen in Figure 2, where different entities are (automatically) placed in the appropriate areas on the screen and color coded. This facilitates learning because secondary notations (Petre & Green, 1993) of placement and color are constant, and easily learned by the students. Again, this semantic knowledge is built into the software tool and requires no effort on the part of the instructor.

Why is program animation so important? The reason is that programs are static representations of complex dynamic processes that take place within the processor and memory of a computer. The student must develop a mental model (Ben-Ari & Yeshno, 2006) of how the program is executed. A mental model is a cognitive structure that a person uses to un-

58

derstand a technological artifact. What distinguishes mental modes from other cognitive structures is that a mental model is *run* by the person in order to explain the behavior of the artifact. Even more important, a mental model can be run to predict the response of the artifact to the person's action.

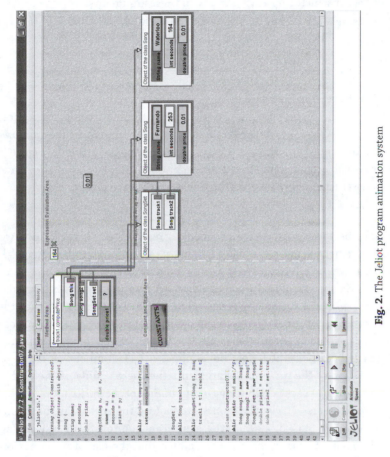

Fig. 2. The Jeliot program animation system

The importance of program animation

Let us look at an example. Currently, a methodology called object-oriented programming (OOP) is being taught to novices and even the simplest OOP program gives rise to complex computation when executed. Consider just the act of creating an object (called a constructor in OOP); the Java code is a single line like:

```
Song song1 = new Song("Waterloo", 164, 0.01);
```

The three parameters to the constructor are the name of the song, its length in seconds, and the price to buy it from an online music service.

59

The steps that must be executed are:

- Allocate memory for the variable `song1`.
- Allocate memory for a new object of class `Song`.
- Evaluate the arguments `"Waterloo"`, `164`, `0.01`.
- Call the constructor for class `Song` with these arguments.
- Allocate memory for the parameters and local variables.
- Initialize the parameters and local variables.
- Execute the statements of the constructor.
- Return a reference to the object.
- Assign the reference to `song1`.

Each of these steps is quite non-trivial in terms of the computation and memory allocation involved. Jeliot can fully animate these actions without any intervention on the part of the teacher or student. Figure 2 shows two objects of class `Song` and one of class `SongSet` after they have been constructed, together with the references to each object.

Research on students using Jeliot

We have performed extensive pedagogical research on Jeliot, which we summarize here. A more extensive summary can be found in Ben-Ari et al. (2011), as well as references to the original publications.

First, we showed that the use of Jeliot significantly improves learning, because it provides a concrete (graphic) vocabulary of terms that the students easily adopt for referring to the dynamic aspects of program execution that are hidden within the computer. In this aspect, Jeliot is superior to Scratch, because Scratch does not support visualization or animation of the execution of the program's statements themselves, only of the visible rendering of the execution in terms of animation of the sprites.

In early studies of visualization systems (see the review in Hundhausen, Douglas, & Stasko, 2002), little significant improvement in learning was observed, but many researchers claimed that the use of visualization improved affective aspects like motivation. We decided to check if the use of Jeliot improved attention under the assumption that attention is a prerequisite for learning. In an experiment with hyperactive students, Jeliot did in fact lead to complete attention to the animation with no disruptive behavior. Of course, one can't expect this level of attention to continue indefinitely when using the software, but it does justify the use of pedagogical software like Jeliot even when learning improvement has not been shown.

The facilities for interaction with Jeliot are limited to entering the source code and program data, and to controlling the nature and rate of the animation (continuous, step-by-step, etc.). In an environment of collaborative learning, the amount of collaboration was positively corollated with the level of engagement. This would justify modifying Jeliot to increase the level of engagement. Alternatively, new tools like UUhistle can be developed. UUhistle engages the student by requiring him/her to simulate the execution of a program on a computer.

Research on teachers using Jeliot

In spite of its proven advantages, we experienced frustration when trying to introduce the use of Jeliot into high-school computer science classes. While many teachers used Jeliot enthusiastically, many others did not. A study of the teachers using phenomenography (Marton & Booth, 1997) turned up a four-category outcome space that was more extensive than we initially expected:

- Appropriation: Jeliot is experienced as a useful tool consistent with the teacher's pedagogical style.

- By-the-book: Jeliot is experienced as a possibly useful tool, but it may not fit with the teacher's pedagogical style.

- Repudiation: Jeliot is experienced as an externally imposed tool of limited usefulness for teaching.

- Dissonant: Jeliot is experienced in a conflicting manner – on the one hand with enthusiasm, and on the other with a reluctance to actually use it.

    The Dissonant category seems rather strange, so we decided to investigate the issue further, using the theory of planned behavior (Ajzen, 1991), which is used to study the connection between attitudes and intentions and from intentions to behavior. This investigation turned up the surprising result that many teachers had a low level of perceived behavioral control (Ajzen, 2002). This means that the teachers were uncertain of their ability to control the use of the Jeliot software in their classroom and its effect on their teaching. The exceptions are those teachers in the Appropriation category, who fully understand the tool and devise the appropriate ways of integrating it into their teaching.

Pedagogical implications

Proficiency in programming. I believe that there is no doubt that educational technology can improve learning, either directly or by increasing affective aspects like attention and self-efficacy. We observed students constructing highly sophisticated software using Scratch, including games and simulations. To do this, they must have achieved a high level of proficiency in using the programming constructs of Scratch. Despite its playful exterior, Scratch is a very advanced programming platform including such features as events, message passing, and concurrency that are usually only taught at the university level. Furthermore, we are currently looking into the transition that middle-school students undergo when they leave Scratch for programming in Java or C# in high schools. Preliminary evidence shows that they easily transfer the knowledge they have gained from visual programming to textual programming.

Development of viable mental modes. The Jeliot program animation system has proved to be highly successful in improving the learning of programming. Our research showed that the average students using Jeliot were able to achieve levels of understanding normally only seen in above-average students. They did this because the visualization software provided a concrete vocabulary of terms in which to express the execution of a computer program. This in turn led to the development of viable mental models that enabled the students to understand how a program is executed. Together with these significant advantages, we encountered some pitfalls that must be considered when introducing educational technology and that go beyond the specific subject of learning programming.

Looking is not seeing. Petre and Green (1993) showed that graphics are not self-explanatory, contrary to the often repeated slogan that "one picture is worth a thousand words". Looking at a picture of an elephant probably gives one a good idea of what an elephant looks like, but when we consider visual software like Scratch and Jeliot, we see that they use abstract representations. For example, Scratch blocks have a complex semantics that is not always apparent from their shape and certainly not from their color, so the student must learn the semantics separately. In Jeliot, all areas of memory are represented by rectangles, so the student must learn the difference between the stack and the heap from the teacher or textbook. Even if memory in the stack and the heap were represented using different shapes, the shapes would have no relationship with the different methods that are used to allocate and de-allocate memory from these areas. The conclusion is that visualization software cannot stand on its own; textbooks or other learning materials and lectures or other teaching opportunities must be provided.

Learning with educational technology has side effects. Just as a student can develop a misconception from a lecture or a textbook, misconceptions can arise from the use of educational technology. This was most apparent in the bad habits of programming that we saw with Scratch. Because Scratch makes it so easy to construct programs by dragging and dropping blocks, the programming process became sloppy with no attempt to design a program's structure. The students placed blocks that they didn't even need and created dozens or even hundreds of short scripts that made the programs difficult, if not impossible, to maintain. In another research project (Ragonis & Ben-Ari, 2005), we used the BlueJ environment mentioned earlier in an introductory course on OOP for novices. We found that because BlueJ enables interactive execution of small parts of the program, students began to treat it like a video game and did not understand the concept of a "program" that executes from start to finish. We had to change the syllabus to overcome this misconception. The lesson is that educational technology must be research-based so that such side effects can be discovered during the period of active development.

Nothing is more important than the teachers. Current trends in education advocate approaches like inquiry learning that are student-centric. However, time after time, we found that the manipulative facility that students easily develop does not often translate into meaningful learning. In learning to program, activities such as understanding the requirements, careful design, documentation, and reflection do not come naturally to students, and only a committed teacher can bring about engagement in these activities that are so necessary in this field.

Educational software is about more than software. There are also implications for the developers of educational technologies. It is not enough for a software system to be effective and easy to use; it must be accompanied by learning materials that will enable teachers to feel comfortable with the software and to smooth the way toward the initial steps of integrating it in their practice.

Implications for teacher professional development. A corollary of the important place of the teacher in the learning process is that the teacher must be highly trained, both in general in the subject matter and specifically in the particular tool being used. Integrating educational technology into one's teaching (what we called Appropriation) is very difficult and requires both significant knowledge of computer systems and a serious commitment by the teacher. Even in an ideal world where all teachers have degrees in computer science, the rapid change of computing technology requires continual updating of the teachers' knowledge. This implies that resources must be allocated for frequent professional development

63

and these resources must include sufficient relief from teaching duties so that teachers can participate in courses and practice on their own. This is much more important when the teacher does not have adequate background in computer science, a common situation in middle schools and even high schools.

A commitment to adapting educational technology is difficult to obtain because teachers must be convinced that the benefits far outweigh the effort to learn new tools and integrate them into their practice. This commitment is extremely fragile since the teachers do not have the time to "debug" technical and pedagogical problems that arise. Therefore, it is essential that sufficient support be available, not just during professional development courses, but also routinely during the school year. If not, the integration of technology into a teacher's practice will not take place and the use of the technology will remain sub-optimal.

Conclusions

The conclusions that are drawn from this line of research are of no surprise. Pedagogical software tools and creative activities by students cannot "replace" the teacher, as one might infer from an extreme interpretation of the doctrine of constructionism (Harel & Papert, 1991) or any similar doctrine where students are supposed to learn by doing with little or no supervision by their teachers. In the case of Scratch, only teachers can teach good programming habits and the principles of program design. In the case of Java and Jeliot, only teachers can decide how to use the tool in order to achieve better learning of a complex programming language. The main implication for the professional development of teachers is that they need to have a deep understanding of the subject matter of informatics in addition to pedagogical methods. Without professional knowledge of the subject they will lack the confidence necessary to optimally use software tools in pedagogical ways.

References

Ajzen, I. (1991). The theory of planned behavior. *Organizational Behavior and Human Decision Processes*, 50(2), 179–211.

Ajzen, I. (2002). Perceived behavioral control, self-efficacy, locus of control, and the theory of planned behavior. *Journal of Applied Social Psychology*, 32(4), 665–683.

Armoni, M., & Ben-Ari, M. (2010). *Computer science concepts through Scratch*. Rehovot, Israel: Weizmann Institute of Science (in Hebrew). Retrieved December 5, 2012, from http://stwww.weizmann.ac.il/g-cs/scratch/learning_book.html

Baecker, R. (1998). Sorting out sorting: A case study of software visualization for teaching computer science. In J. Stasko et al. (Eds.), *Software visualization: Programming as a multimedia experience* (pp. 369–381). Cambridge, MA: MIT Press.

Visualization of programming

Ben-Ari, M., Bednarik, R., Ben-Bassat Levy, R., Ebel, G., Moreno, A., Myller, N., & Sutinen, E. (2011). A decade of research and development on program animation: The Jeliot experience. *Journal of Visual Languages and Computing*, 22(5), 275–384.

Ben-Ari, M., & Yeshno, T. (2006). Conceptual models of software artifacts. *Interacting with Computers*, 18(6), 1336–1350.

Dann, W., Cooper, S., & Pausch, R. (2009). *Learning to program with Alice*. Upper Saddle River, NJ: Pearson.

Eisenstadt, M., & Brayshaw, M. (1988). The Transparent Prolog Machine (TPM): An execution model and graphical debugger for logic programming. *Journal of Logic Programming*, 5(4), 277–342.

Harel, I., & Papert, S. (Eds.). (1991). *Constructionism*. Norwood, NJ: Ablex.

Hundhausen, C. D., Douglas, S. A., & Stasko J. T. (2002). A meta-study of algorithm visualization effectiveness. *Journal of Visual Languages and Computing*, 13(3), 259–290.

Kelleher, C., & Pausch, R. (2005). Lowering the barriers to programming: A taxonomy of programming environments and languages for novice programmers. *ACM Computing Surveys*, 37(2), 83–137.

Marton, F., & Booth, S. A. (1997). *Learning and awareness*. Mahwah, NJ: Lawrence Erlbaum.

Meerbaum-Salant, O., Armoni, M., & Ben-Ari, M. (2010). Learning computer science concepts with Scratch. In *Proceedings of the Sixth International Workshop on Computing Education Research*, Aarhus, Denmark, August 2010 (pp. 69–76). New York: ACM.

Meerbaum-Salant, O., Armoni, M., & Ben-Ari, M. (2011). Habits of programming in Scratch. In *Proceedings of the Sixteenth SIGCSE Conference on Innovation and Technology in Computer Science Education*, Darmstadt, Germany, June 2011 (pp. 168–172). New York: ACM.

Petre, M., & Green, T. R. G. (1993). Learning to read graphics: Some evidence that 'seeing' an information display is an acquired skill. *Journal of Visual Languages and Computing*, 4(1), 55–70.

Price, B., Baecker, R., & Small, I. (1998). An introduction to software visualization. In J. Stasko et al. (Eds.), *Software visualization: Programming as a multimedia experience* (pp. 3–27). Cambridge, MA: MIT Press.

Ragonis, N., & Ben-Ari, M. (2005). A long-term investigation of the comprehension of OOP concepts by novices. *Computer Science Education*, 15(3), 203–221.

Repenning, A., & Sumner, T. (1995). Agentsheets: A medium for creating domain-oriented visual languages. *IEEE Computer*, 28(3), 17–25.

Resnick, M., Maloney, J., Monroy-Hernández, A., Rusk, N., Eastmond, E., Brennan, K., Millner, A., Rosenbaum, E., Silver, J., Silverman, B., & Kafai, Y. (2009). Scratch: Programming for all. *Communications of the ACM*, 52(11), 60–67.

Shaffer, C. A., Cooper, M. L., Alon, A. D. J., Akbar, M., Stewart, M., Ponce, S., & Edwards, S. H. (2010). Algorithm visualization: The state of the field. *ACM Transactions on Computing Education*, 10(3), Article 9.

Sorva, J., & Sirkiä, T. (2010). UUhistle: A software tool for visual program simulation. In *Proceedings of the 10th Koli Calling International Conference on Computing Education Research*, Koli, Finland, November 2010 (pp. 49–54). New York: ACM.

Stasko, J., Domingue, J. Brown, M. H., & Price, B. A. (Eds.). (1998). *Software visualization: Programming as a multimedia experience*. Cambridge, MA: MIT Press.

5

UNPLUGGING
COMPUTER SCIENCE

Tim Bell and Heidi Newton

Introduction

Computer Science Unplugged (also known as "CS Unplugged" or just "Unplugged") is an approach to communicating some of the great ideas of computer science without requiring students to use a computer (Bell et al., 2009). It has become very popular internationally as a tool for outreach, as students can be introduced in less than an hour to a topic such as coding, graph algorithms, artificial intelligence, algorithm complexity, or tractability. The students engage with the topic by being given a challenge or puzzle that forces them to think through the issues that computer scientists grapple with.

A simple example of an Unplugged activity is the "Parity Trick," which is presented as a magic trick that can lead to exploration of error-correcting codes. The trick can be done with a set of square cards that are black on one side and white on the other. A student is asked to lay out cards in a five by five grid, with a random mix of white and black showing. The "magician" then says "actually, I'm going to make it a bit harder" and adds extra squares to make the grid six by six. Another student is then asked to flip over one of the cards while the magician looks the other way. The magician then tells the class which card was flipped. The secret behind the trick (which students are led through a constructivist process to discover) is that the magician used the extra cards to ensure there was an even number of black cards in each row, so they simply had to look for the row and column with an odd number of black cards to identify the flipped card.

The trick is very motivating for students – they want to know how it is done – and once they have deduced the method, they have effectively constructed an error-correcting code, which can lead to discussions on the importance of such codes when computer data is stored and transmitted. Depending on the maturity of the students and the context of the class, they can then explore questions such as how the system deals with multiple errors, and the difference between error correction and error detection. In the big picture, the main thing they are learning is that there are techniques in computer science that are simple enough that they could understand them, and are interesting, important, and often invisible to computer users. The goal of the parity activity is not that students would then know how to do error correction, but simply that they would be aware that the problem exists and it has clever solutions, which in turn raise new questions (such as what types of errors are likely).

Another benefit of the Unplugged activities is that they are generally very kinesthetic, and get the students away from the computer, providing a break from typing and staring at a screen. This in turn can lead to more social activities, group problem solving, and more engagement of students.

The Unplugged activities cover many areas of computer science, providing opportunities to expose students to the richness of the topic, and defining the discipline by giving meaningful examples. In general the list of topics is based on the ACM Computer Science Curriculum (acm.org/education/curricula-recommendations) that guides colleges and universities on the topics in a computer science degree, attempting to give a representative coverage of the topics so that students have a broad picture. Of course, different definitions of computer science are used in different contexts, but the Unplugged material can be used selectively as appropriate.

There is plenty of material available for using Unplugged for computer science outreach, particularly the detailed activities, videos, and other resources at the main CS Unplugged website (csunplugged.org). There are also several reports on using it on various outreach programs, including school visits (Groover, 2009; Hart, Early, & Brylow, 2008) and camps (Carmichael, 2008; Lambert & Guiffre, 2009). It is also valuable as part of conventional classroom teaching, but the activities need to be adapted. Thies and Vahrenhold (2012) point out that a key element that is needed is learning objectives, and they extract objectives for Unplugged activities.

In this chapter we explain the rationale for using the Unplugged approach, and then give examples of how it can be used for both junior and senior school classes. We provide some general principles for applying the approach to the classroom, and conclude with some recommendations for teacher professional development as preparation to use Unplugged as part of one's teaching.

Rationale for unplugging computer science

The name "computer science" is widely misunderstood in school systems, and often confused with subjects like ICT and IT, and can be assumed to simply mean learning to use computers. For example, a recent Royal Society report in the UK says that "a negative experience of digital literacy within ICT can sometimes put students off pursuing computer science or lead to a misunderstanding of what computer science 'is' " (Furber, 2012 p. 15). In other places the subject is confused with programming (which is indeed fundamental to computer science, but not exclusively what the subject is about). For example, until recently the main Advanced Placement exam in computer science in the USA has been on Java programming. Computer Science Unplugged is an approach originally designed for use in outreach programs for school students to address these issues by giving a better understanding of what the topic is. Many Unplugged activities are publicly available on the main website (csunplugged.org), including videos that demonstrate how they can be used with students.

A key element of Computer Science Unplugged is to provide tools for enabling students to engage with big ideas in computer science without having to learn to program first. Often programming can be a "gateway" to getting into computer science, and the goal of Unplugged is to provide students with a vision of what lies past that barrier, and to find out if they are interested in the topic. We have also found that it is valuable to do computer science away from a computer because the computer can become a distraction – if programming is the focus of learning then students start focusing on details (like how to represent the problem in a programming language) or issues that arise (such as tracking down a tricky bug in a program) rather than thinking about the big ideas and thinking in an algorithmic way, which are indeed very important skills in our digital world.

Unplugged is also valuable as a tool for exposing students to exciting advanced topics (such as graph theory) where there are open problems to be explored, rather than focusing only on routine techniques such as how HTML works (Bell et al., 2012).The idea is to inspire students rather than simply train them to carry out routine well-defined tasks.

One idea that permeates the use of Unplugged activities is taking a socio-constructivist approach – an Unplugged activity provides the scaffolding to approach a problem. This approach to teaching is based on Piaget's constructivist theory, that students *construct* knowledge in their mind rather than having it transferred from a teacher. Thus, providing them with a social context where they are guided through experiences to enable this construction to happen is a powerful way of teaching (Bransford et al., 2000). The idea of "scaffolding" is to provide enough guidance (in Unplugged, typically through the brief rules of an activity) to enable them to start constructing new knowledge that builds on their current knowledge and skills. Often this is done by using a story that makes the constraints clear – for example, in the muddy city problem where the mayor must minimize the number of roads that need to be paved to connect all the houses. However, students should not be told how to solve the problem – returning to the muddy city activity, Kruskal's algorithm is a simple approach that gives an optimal solution, and many students are capable of discovering this themselves, so to tell them the algorithm would be to rob them of the opportunity to explore the problem and possible solutions. Allowing them to experiment with different algorithms means that they are constructing their knowledge by evaluating different approaches; simply giving them the "correct" algorithm means that they might now know a solution to one particular problem, but they haven't been through the process of solving the problem, and have missed out on developing skills that can be of value to them in future situations.

As another example, in the searching activity students need to try to "find" their opponent's battleship, and (for example) when the numbers are sorted into order it would be tempting for the teacher to suggest that students try the middle one first (which is the binary search strategy). However, to allow them to construct that knowledge, they should be allowed to try whatever choice they come up with; many will reason that the middle one is a good choice anyway, but those that don't will learn from the experience that they made a suboptimal choice, thus constructing the algorithm for themselves rather than having it given to them. The challenge is for the teacher to guide students through the activities in a way that enables them to discover solutions for themselves.

Example using Unplugged for younger students: Binary numbers

The following example shows a way to teach binary representation of numbers using a constructivist approach. The sequence of instructions is taken from a version of the Unplugged activity on binary numbers, and is suitable for younger middle-school students (in fact, this version only requires students to be able to count to 31, and has been used in a similar form for 5-year-old students).

The general approach is to give each student the five cards shown in the table below, and give them the simple rule that each card can be either completely visible (dots showing) or not visible (flipped over). Students are then given challenges such as flipping over cards to make exactly 5 dots visible (in this case the 4 and 1 card need to be shown). The layout of cards corresponds to the binary number for 5 (00101), where a 0 means the card is hidden and a 1 means it is visible. Through this simple scaffolding relatively young students can perform conversions from binary to decimal and back; more importantly, they can reason about the process instead of simply learning a given algorithm.

The commentary below explains the steps of the activity in terms of educational theory. Socio-constructivism (already mentioned) emphasizes having students construct their own knowledge. We also use Vygotsky's "Zone of Proximal Development" (ZDP) (Bransford et al., 2000), which is concerned with keeping the student in a zone where they are building on what they already know, avoiding being above this zone (where they get frustrated because they don't have the basics to understand the material) or below it (where they would be bored because they are only exercising what they already are competent at). We also refer to Bloom's taxonomy as revised by Anderson and Krathwohl (Anderson et al., 2001), which is concerned with the different levels of cognitive objectives that range from simply remembering or understanding facts through applying the knowledge, and at the higher level using it to analyze, evaluate, and create.

In the following the questions that the teacher asks are shown in *italics*, and the commentary is interspersed.

(a)   (b)

Fig. 1. (a) The binary cards (b) Showing the number 5

Put the five cards on the table in front of you, in the order shown (Fig. 1a).

In terms of Vygotsky's ZDP, the cards are the scaffolding for the students' learning. The assumption is that the students can count the number of dots on the cards, and copy this pattern. These skills are fairly basic, and the scaffolding is suitable for very young school children.

What do you notice about the number of dots on the cards?

This is a constructive step: We're asking students to notice the doubling from left to right. We could have simply told the students "each card is double the number of dots of the one to its right," but this would push their learning to the lower end of Bloom's taxonomy (remembering) rather than understanding, or even analyzing.

How many dots would the next card have if we added a 6th card on to the left?

This is a chance to test what the student inferred in the previous step: It exercises their understanding of the scaffolding, and has them applying their new knowledge.

How many dots would there be if we added yet another card on the left?

This reinforces the student's understanding from the previous step.

We can use these cards to represent numbers by turning some of them face down and adding up the number of dots that are showing. The rule is that each card is either fully visible, or fully hidden. How can you have exactly 5 dots showing?

This is additional scaffolding, providing a simple rule (cards are visible or not) and a goal (to show 5 dots). Taking a constructivist approach, the students are not told any more; they need to experiment to solve the problem. They will discover for themselves that some cards (e.g. the 16) are too big to be useful, and some (e.g. the 4) are essential to make up the number. The solution is shown in Figure 1b.

This approach has students working at a higher level of Bloom's taxonomy (arguably they are creating an algorithm); if they had been given a method for the conversion, then they would be working at a low level, and wouldn't have the same level of understanding, and more importantly, might not develop the confidence that they could come up with their own algorithms.

The activity continues with questions such as working out other values, representing the cards using zeros and ones, determining the smallest value that can be represented (0, not 1), and having students count from 0 to 31 on the cards. If the teacher asks the right questions along the way, students can discover patterns: For example, if all the cards are showing then the number of dots can be calculated as one less than the number of dots that would be on the next card to be added; and that there is only one way to represent each number.

This binary coding example uses a well-understood concept, and relatively young students are capable of discovering a reliable algorithm for decimal to binary conversion. Some of the Unplugged activities introduce ideas that are not well understood, are open problems, or have challenging issues, such as finding solutions for NP-complete problems or determining if a computer program is "intelligent." By exploring such problems students learn what is involved in the boundaries of our understanding, and more importantly, discover that computer science isn't a closed set of solved problems, but a treasure trove of questions and opportunities, some of which they may well make new discoveries about one day. But most importantly, they learn that computer science is an exciting discipline, and not just a collection of low-level routine knowledge such as how to format pages in a word processor, or how to make tables in HTML.

Example for older students: Sorting algorithms

The following sorting algorithm activity is more suitable for older students; it has been used in classes for 15-year old students in New Zealand to teach the idea of algorithmic complexity without having to be able to write programs or use the traditional big O notation.

Fig. 2. Sorting weights using a scale (taken from youtube.com/watch?v=cVMKXKoGu_Y)

The key to the activity (scaffolding) is to have a set of weights that look identical (e.g., film canisters with differing amounts of coins or sand in them), which can be compared in pairs using a balance scale, as shown in Figure 2. This simulates a typical sorting algorithm where a binary comparison operation is used on values, and it prevents students being able to see the ordering at a glance. The activity can either be done by one student in front of the class (with guidance from the class), or by groups or individual students each with their own balance scale. A typical sequence of instructions using a constructivist approach goes as follows (this example assumes that there are 11 weights, as shown in Figure 2):

1. Choose two weights, and find out which is the heaviest. (This gets the student used to using the scale to compare two weights.)
2. Now try to find the heaviest weight of the whole set. (With relatively little guidance students should be able to work out that they leave the

heaviest one where it is on the scale, and compare another one from the set with it, retaining the heaviest one each time.)

3. Ask how many comparisons are required to find the heaviest one. (This can even be done before the student doing the demonstration has finished finding it, as students should be able to predict that ten comparisons will be made, one for each weight except the first one chosen.) Initially some may guess 11 comparisons, one for each weight, but they should be able to explain to each other why it is only ten.

4. Now introduce the idea that we want to sort the weights into order from lightest to heaviest. Point out that the heaviest one has been found, and can be placed in its correct place on the right. Ask what we might do next (or if more guidance is needed, how could we find the second heaviest weight?). Students will usually quickly realize that the same method (algorithm) can be applied to the remaining ten weights.

5. Before the heaviest of the ten is found, ask how many comparisons (weighings) will be needed. From the previous experience, students should quickly realize that it is nine.

6. The students can then complete the exercise in one of two ways: They can count the number of weighings needed to sort all the weights into order (empirical evaluation), or they can work out that it will take $10+9+8+7+6+5+4+3+2+1$ comparisons, and simply add up the numbers. This highlights how some algorithms can be analyzed without even implementing them; it is common for students to be able to work out the total (55) faster than they could do it empirically. Some students may know the trick where the sequence of numbers can be doubled up and added in reverse, i.e., $(10+1)+(9+2)+(8+3)+(7+4)+(6+5)+(5+6)+(4+7)+(3+8)+(2+9)+(1+10) = 10 \times 11$, so the total is a half of 110, or 55.

7. Now ask the students to estimate how many comparisons would be required to sort 110 weights (ten times as many). They will typically estimate ten times the effort is required, i.e., 550 comparisons, which is incorrect. Now have them apply what they have just learned by first asking how many comparisons will be made to find the heaviest of 110 weights (it is 109 comparisons, one less than the number of weights; they will probably know this general rule by now). Thus the total is $109+108+108+\ldots+1$, which using the trick above is $110 \times 109 / 2 = 5995$.

It is important to have them realize the significance of this; ten times the size of input takes more than 100 times as many comparisons. Mathematically experienced students may know or deduce the general formula for sorting n items this way as $n(n-1)/2$ comparisons. The dominating value in this formula is n^2, that is, the sorting algorithm does not scale well as the time taken will increase quadratically with the size of the input.

A key point that we want students to have constructed for themselves from this is that having ten times as much data may take a lot more than ten times as long to process. In the context of a successful business, using this algorithm could mean that going from 1,000 customers to 10,000 customers will make their computer system run 100 times slower, or that they need a computer 100 times as fast even though they only have ten times as many customers to pay for it. This algorithm isn't sustainable as the size of the input gets larger and larger, and a better algorithm is needed instead.

The full CS Unplugged activity for sorting shows the teacher how to get the students to compare the above algorithm (called selection sort) with a much more efficient one (quicksort). Doing quicksort using balance scales is fairly easy even for young children, but analyzing it isn't so simple. Nevertheless, students can do experiments with specific examples of the two algorithms to compare them (in the video shown in Figure 2, quicksort happens to be about twice as fast). The difference between these two algorithms isn't always obvious with a few items, but becomes quite extreme with large numbers of values being sorted. For this students might download a program for each method (some are available on the website nzacditt.org.nz/resources that can show the number of comparisons for large numbers of items being sorted), or run a simulation in an online visualization (e.g., sorting-algorithms.com), and compare how long they take for various sizes of input. With this approach students don't need to be able to write a program, yet they can experience first-hand that there is significantly more than a constant factor difference between two different approaches to a problem.

This particular example counters the idea that computers are so fast these days that it doesn't matter what algorithm you use. In contrast, choosing a good algorithm is essential to making sure that a system is scalable, and some systems have been victims of their own success because they can't cope with large numbers of users and/or large amounts of data.

Unplugged in the classroom

The above examples illustrate how the Unplugged activities can be used in a classroom situation. They are a little different from the original outreach activities because they have specific objectives; in the first case the implicit objective is that students should be able to perform decimal to binary conversions, and be aware of the limits of the coding; and in the second one, the objective is that students can appreciate that an algorithm can sometimes be analyzed, and that two different algorithms for the same task can have considerably different performance.

Using the originally published Unplugged activities without linking them to objectives can detract from the impact of the approach in the classroom. In fact, researchers who have tried to use Unplugged in its original form without adapting it sufficiently to the particular group in the classroom have reported that it is less effective than might be expected. Taub et al. (Taub, Armoni, & Ben-Ari, 2012; Taub, Ben-Ari, & Armoni, 2009) noted that the Unplugged activities need to be adapted for the age group (for example, the binary numbers above assume fairly elementary math skills, and older students could work with more cards, and numbers instead of dots), and that practical links need to be made to concepts in computer science (for example, the sorting activity above is interesting in itself, but some effort is needed to draw out the idea that sorting algorithms are used in real life). Feaster et al. (2011) report similar issues, where the original Unplugged activities (written for primary school children) appeared to have little impact on high-school age students, possibly because the students viewed themselves as already expert in the subject, and also were less interested in kinesthetic activities. This reflects our experience, where the "mood" of a class can make a big difference between whether they eagerly participate or try to distance themselves, or even undermine the activity. In contrast, primary school students are much more eager to explore, experiment, and participate. With older students, the teacher needs to be a lot more agile to adapt the pace to the class, bearing in mind that the object is to achieve the learning objective and not to slavishly complete each instruction in the Unplugged activity step by step. For example, with the binary number activity older students may quickly latch on to the conversion method, and will only be bored if they have to complete all the worksheets provided.

Thies and Vahrenhold (2012) had more success with Unplugged by identifying learning objectives for the activities, and mapping them on to an adapted Bloom's taxonomy so that the teacher could be aware of the learning that each activity could be used for. This also enables the teacher to develop assessment so that they can evaluate if students have achieved the objectives; for older students especially, assessment of objectives can be a bigger motivator than the enjoyment of participating in the activity.

One way to achieve this is to use an Unplugged activity as a brief warm-up or introduction, and then have students write programs that implement the concept in the activity. Moti Ben-Ari has released a series of Scratch programs that demonstrate how this might be done (available from code.google.com/p/scratch-unplugged).

As an example of a different form of follow-up, in the recently adopted New Zealand computer science standards (Bell, Andreae, & Lambert, 2010; Bell, Andreae, & Robins, 2012), one of the requirements for students at Year 12 (second to last year of high school) is to compare different ways of representing the same type of data using bits, and to discuss the implications of each representation. The way the assessment is done is that students are required to write a report, rather than sit an exam, so a particular challenge is to make sure that students can report on a personal experience with the concept, and not just reproduce standard material from a textbook or online.

A way to introduce the idea that text can be represented using bits is to initially consider an artificial system that represents the 26 letters of the alphabet in lowercase. Students can be given a message and the objective of finding a simple way to represent it in binary. As long as they have a good understanding of binary numbers, they can be guided quite quickly to using five bits per letter, simply assigning binary numbers in the form of $a = 1$, $b = 2$, $c = 3$, etc. They can then consider ideas such as whether leading zeroes matter, how the computer finds the start of a character, and whether or not this system would be suitable for real-world use. The Unplugged "modem" exercise provides opportunities to practice this coding (csunplugged.org/modem). After this, if the students are given an ASCII table and then a Unicode table, minimal explanation will be required for them to understand as they can apply what they figured out for themselves in the artificial example. This sets them up to be able to successfully compare the three systems using their own understanding, demonstrating the encodings using their own messages.

Another requirement at the New Zealand year 12 high-school level is that students evaluate a widely used system that uses a form of encoding, such as error control coding. In this case, the Parity Trick (described in the introduction) can be used as a brief warm-up. Because of the constructivist approach, students will have figured out for themselves that error correction is both possible and has important applications. To extend them, they can answer questions such as "what if two cards were flipped?", "what if the flipped cards were in the same row?", "what if more cards were flipped?", and "in which cases can the errors simply be detected and in which can they be reliably corrected?" Answering, explaining, and justifying such questions with their own examples allows them to evaluate an error-correcting code.

Alternatively, the questions above can be answered as part of a class discussion, and students can then be sent away to investigate another system independently, such as check digits in ISBN book numbers, bar codes, or credit card numbers. Information on these follow-up exercises is available on the Unplugged website on the page for the Parity Trick. The follow-up can in turn can lead to using a spreadsheet to calculate the check digit given a number, and students can efficiently experiment with different types of errors (number substitutions, transpositions, etc.).

The approaches described above not only have the student actively engaging with the concept, but they also provide a level of authenticity in project work. In the New Zealand context, where students are typically expected to turn in a project with requirements such as "Showing an understanding of error-correcting codes," a significant issue is that students are tempted to demonstrate their understanding by writing about what the teacher said and what various websites said, sometimes even resorting to paraphrasing websites without necessarily understanding what they are paraphrasing. This can be avoided if the students base their explanations around personalized examples that nobody else in the class would have used, for example, showing the calculation of the checksum of the ISBN for their favorite book, and the bar code for their favorite food. This helps ensure that students didn't copy one another and also encourages the use of the "student voice" in their explanations; the student is writing about what *they* discovered based on their own exploration and experiments as opposed to what the teacher or Wikipedia said. In the context of Bloom's taxonomy, the students have essentially gone from lower levels (remembering and understanding) to higher levels (evaluating and analyzing).

Because Unplugged is based around activities and exploring as opposed to lengthy explanations, it lends itself well to this style of learning and assessment. Instead of using standard examples, students could demonstrate character coding by writing their own name or a word that is significant to them using binary; with the parity cards there are 2^{25} (33,554,432) possible layouts to demonstrate (although a few are too trivial), and for sorting, there are 11! (39,916,800) permutations of input that might have been used to demonstrate the algorithm. Contrasting these personalized demonstrations with a project that paraphrases standard texts and websites, we see that a student can demonstrate understanding without using jargon, and using jargon doesn't necessarily demonstrate understanding.

Professional development

There are many ideas available for using Computer Science Unplugged in the classroom, and most of these can be accessed through the Unplugged website (csunplugged.org) and the references at the end of this chapter. The Unplugged approach has been used all around the world (the material has been translated into over 15 languages), and the website collects ideas that others have contributed for adapting the approaches for their cultures and contexts. In New Zealand this approach has been used for teaching some of the topics introduced in a revised set of standards introduced in 2011. The approach has been used earlier in South Korea (Choi et al., 2008; Yoo et al., 2006), and more recently has been used in the USA in courses aimed at high schools as part of the "Passion, Beauty and Joy" computing principles project (Garcia et al., 2012) and the "Exploring Computer Science" (ECS) course (Goode & Margolis, 2011). In the UK it has been used as part of "Computer Science for Fun" (CS4FN), which is an outreach targeting high schools. Unplugged is recommended in the Royal Society report on changing the high-school curriculum (Furber, 2012), and in Scotland is a major part of the "Computing Science Inside" program (Cutts et al., 2007). The US National Center for Women in Technology (NCWIT) has adapted the material and published it as a "promising practice" and also as "Computer Science-in-a-box" (ncwit.org/unplugged). This widespread usage indicates that teachers around the world have recognized it as a worthwhile tool to have in their selection of approaches to teaching computer science, and anyone who has used it first-hand will have experienced the enjoyment that teachers and students experience working on activities. However, it is very important to use the ideas appropriately for the age level and the goals of the group you are working with; an approach that works well with one group can fall flat with another if this isn't taken account of.

As a program of professional development, the following steps can be taken to become familiar with the activities available and to work out how to deploy them in the context of your own classroom.

(1) Review the Computer Science Unplugged videos (available from youtube.com/csunplugged). These have been developed for teachers, so that you can see what some of the activities would look like if used in the classroom. Reviewing these videos provides the opportunity to see how the activities can be applied. They are *not* intended for showing to classes; it is much better for students to do the exercises themselves than to watch others do them (the exception is the "Reaching out" video, which itself is a

puzzle for the students to try to decode). Most of the examples in the videos are just a few minutes, but in practice most activities take 30 to 60 minutes by the time the students participate in the activities themselves, and discuss solutions or challenges that arise from what they have learned.

(2) Read a detailed lesson plan based on the Unplugged approach. As a starting point, there is one available online for one of the computer science standards available in New Zealand (the standard is number AS91371, also known as 2.44, and the plan is available via the website nzacditt.org.nz/resources). The lesson covers several hours of work with students, and provides detailed guidance for a teacher with suggestions of examples to use, projects for students to explore the concepts on a computer once they have understood them offline, and ideas for assessing the students' understanding of the material. The topics covered are Binary Representation (binary numbers, and examples such as codes for colors and ASCII/Unicode), Encryption (using a simple code but considering concepts such as brute force and known plaintext attacks), Error Control Coding (starting with the parity activity, and leading to check digits systems), Compression (comparing how much different compression methods compress different files), and Human Computer Interaction (using heuristics to evaluate an interface).

(3) Look through the other Unplugged computing topics on the website (csunplugged.org) and considering which ones would work in your classroom and within the topics you are teaching. Each topic comes with an activity that is written up in a few pages, but the website also provides links to many follow-up activities and extension ideas, enabling you to decide what would be most suitable for your class. Most of the activities are suitable for relatively young students (they were often developed and tested with students who are in their first few years of school), although some (such as the public key cryptosystem) require mathematic maturity that would be more suitable for students approaching their high-school years. Perhaps surprisingly, some of the activities that young children find exciting are difficult for older students; more "mature" students can lack a sense of curiosity and creativity, and may be used to an environment where they "have to" learn some technique and reproduce it, rather than putting aside a rigid curriculum and exploring ideas purely for the fun of doing so. For this reason, an activity that could be used as a full class for junior students might be just a five-minute warm-up for seniors. It will be important to judge the best way to deploy the ideas in your context.

(4) Prepare an activity to try with a class. You will need to develop learning objectives for the class, and select suitable activities to meet those objectives. The challenge is to approach it by primarily asking them questions, not giving answers. Sometimes students need to be given space to explore, and this can be uncomfortable at first as there may be a lack of progress initially, or students may go off in directions not envisioned. For a good description of this process happening, see Casey (1990). Following the students' lead can be very satisfying once you get to the point that students are discovering ideas for themselves. Set yourself the challenge of seeing how much can they figure out for themselves; they may even discover things that you as the teacher don't know, so be prepared to be a guide as much as a leader.

(5) Perform research on the application of Unplugged in the classroom. There are many issues that could be studied, including the level of engagement of different kinds of learners, how the activities tie into other curricula requirements (including math and science), and the value of the activities for developing collaborative problem solving amongst students.

The Unplugged approach isn't a panacea for computer science education; it is just one tool in the teacher's toolbox that has proven useful in promoting students' learning. It was originally designed as an outreach program, because it enabled deep topics from computer science to be covered in a very short time without students having to learn programming, or even have the distraction of using a computer. However, by applying good pedagogical techniques and adapting the material to the particular context, it can serve as an engaging way to enable students to explore advanced concepts.

References

Anderson, L. W., Krathwohl, D. R., Airasian, P., Cruikshank, K., Mayer, R., Pintrich, P., Raths, J., et al. (2001). *A taxonomy for learning, teaching, and assessing: A revision of Bloom's taxonomy of educational objectives* (abridged edition). New York: Addison Wesley Longman.

Bell, T., Alexander, J., Freeman, I., & Grimley, M. (2009). Computer science unplugged: School students doing real computing without computers. *The NZ Journal of Applied Computing and Information Technology, 13*(1), 20–29.

Bell, T., Andreae, P., & Lambert, L. (2010). Computer science in New Zealand high schools. In T. Clear & J. Hamer (Eds.), *ACE '10: Proceedings of the 12th conference on Australasian computing education* (Vol. 32, pp. 15–22). Brisbane, Australia: Australian Computer Society, Inc.

Bell, T., Andreae, P., & Robins, A. (2012). Computer science in NZ high schools: The first year of the new standards. In L. A. Smith King, D. R. Musicant, T. Camp, & P. Tymann (Eds.), *SIGCSE '12: Proceedings of the 43rd ACM technical symposium on computer science education* (pp. 343–348). New York: ACM.

Bell, T., Fellows, M., Rosamond, F., Bell, J., & Marghitu, D. (2012). Unplugging education: Removing barriers to engaging with new disciplines. *Proceedings of SDPS–12*. Retrieved

December 7, 2012, from http://sdps.omnibooksonline.com/2012/data/papers/168.pdf

Bransford, J. D., Brown, A. L., Cocking, R. R., Donovan, M. S., & Pellegrino, J. W. (Eds.). (2000). *How people learn: Brain, mind, experience, and school.* Washington, DC: National Academy Press. Retrieved December 7, 2012, from www.nap.edu/openbook.php?isbn=0309070368

Carmichael, G. (2008). Girls, computer science, and games. *SIGCSE Bulletin, 40*(4), 107–110.

Casey, N. (1990). Whole language: Lessons for math teachers. Retrieved December 7, 2012, from wwwc3.lanl.gov/mega-math/papers/firest.ps

Choi, S. K., Bell, T., Jun, S. J., & Lee, W. G. (2008). Designing offline computer science activities for the Korean elementary school curriculum. In J. Amillo, C. Laxer, E. M. Ruiz, & A. Young (Eds.), *ITiCSE 08: Proceedings of the 13th annual conference on innovation and technology in computer science education* (p. 338). New York: ACM.

Cutts, Q. I., Brown, M. I., Kemp, L., & Matheson, C. (2007). Enthusing and informing potential computer science students and their teachers. In J. Hughes, D. R. Peiris, & P. T. Tymann (Eds.), *ITiCSE 07: Proceedings of the 12th Annual SIGCSE conference on innovation and technology in computer science education* (pp. 196–200). New York: ACM.

Feaster, Y., Segars, L., Wahba, S. K., & Hallstrom, J. O. (2011). Teaching CS unplugged in the high school (with limited success). In G. Rößling, T. L. Naps, & C. Spannagel (Eds.), *ITiCSE 2011: Proceedings of the 16th Annual SIGCSE conference on innovation and technology in computer science education* (pp. 248–252). New York: ACM.

Furber, S. (Ed.). (2012). *Shut down or restart? The way forward for computing in UK schools.* London: The Royal Society. Retrieved December 7, 2012, from http://royalsociety.org/education/policy/computing-in-schools/report/

Garcia, D., Ericson, B., Goode, J., & Lewis, C. (2012). Rediscovering the passion, beauty, joy, and awe: Making computing fun again, part 5. In L. A. Smith King, D. R. Musicant, T. Camp, & P. Tymann (Eds.), *SIGCSE '12, Proceedings of the 43rd ACM technical symposium on computer science education* (pp. 577–578). New York: ACM.

Goode, J., & Margolis, J. (2011). Exploring computer science: A case study of school reform. *ACM Transactions on Computing Education, 11*(2), 12:1–12:16.

Groover, T. R. (2009). Using games to introduce middle school girls to computer science. *Journal of Computing Sciences in Colleges, 24*(6), 132–138.

Hart, M., Early, J. P., & Brylow, D. (2008). A novel approach to K-12 CS education: Linking mathematics and computer science. In J. D. Dougherty, S. H. Rodger, S. Fitzgerald, & M. Guzdial (Eds.), *SIGCSE '08: Proceedings of the 39th SIGCSE technical symposium on computer science education* (pp. 286–290). New York: ACM.

Lambert, L., & Guiffre, H. (2009). Computer science outreach in an elementary school. *Journal of Computing Sciences in Colleges, 24*(3), 118–124.

Taub, R., Armoni, M., & Ben-Ari, M. (2012). CS unplugged and middle-school students' views, attitudes, and intentions regarding CS. *ACM Transactions on Computing Education, 12(2),* 1–29.

Taub, R., Ben-Ari, M. (Moti), & Armoni, M. (2009). The effect of CS unplugged on middle-school students' views of CS. *ACM SIGCSE Bulletin, 41*(3), 99–103.

Thies, R., & Vahrenhold, J. (2012). Reflections on outreach programs in CS classes: Learning objectives for "unplugged" activities. In L. A. Smith King, D. R. Musicant, T. Camp, & P. Tymann (Eds.), *SIGCSE '12: Proceedings of the 43rd ACM technical symposium on computer science education* (pp. 487–492). New York: ACM.

Yoo, S., Yeum, Y., Kim, Y., Cha, S., Kim, J., Jang, H., Choi, S., et al. (2006). Development of an integrated informatics curriculum for K-12 in Korea. In R. Mittermeir (Ed.), Informatics education: The bridge between using and understanding computers (pp. 199–208). *Lecture Notes in Computer Science*, Vol. 4226. New York: Springer.

6

ASSESSMENT OF
STUDENTS' PROGRAMS

Valentina Dagiene and Bronius Skupas

Introduction

Assessment is part of the teacher's job. It can focus on the individual learner, the learning community, the institution, or the educational system as a whole. The final purposes and assessment practices in education depend on the theoretical framework of the practitioners and researchers, their assumptions and beliefs about the nature of the human mind, the origin of knowledge, and the process of learning. Assessment is often divided using the following distinctions: formative and summative; objective and subjective; criterion-referenced, norm-referenced, and impassive; informal and formal. Functions of assessment can be different also: assessment to a) give grades (tests the outcome of education), b) give feedback to learners and teachers in order to support the learning process, c) prognoses about future learning and success.

In this chapter, we discuss assessment in teaching informatics, with a focus on assessment of programming as indicator of problem-solving competencies. Problem solving is one of the important issues of teaching and learning today. Is problem-solving in informatics different from that of other sciences? Yes, it is. The main difference is that the student is designing an algorithm (program) following the exact requirements – rules of the game (Mayer, 1991).

Programming is one of the most essential intellectual parts of informatics. However, programming is not an easy job: it requires much effort and specific skills. Programming is a creative process that encourages thinking and the integration of knowledge from various fields. In schools, programming helps form a professional attitude to application, and prompts an impact on implementation in an efficient way. A programming module or course usually ends with an exam or a test. We noticed that the maturity exam, which students can select at the end of secondary education, enhances the subject's visibility and helps to motivate students to choose this subject for studies. Also it is assumed that the programming exam will help some students to become interested in this activity and they will pursue programming as a profession.

Teaching programming influences the development of thinking. Capability of constructing programs (algorithms) helps a student to conceive the technical performance of a computer and forms a conceptual understanding of information technologies. Constructing an algorithm (program) is a discovery for a student, training his/her creative capabilities (Dagiene & Grigas, 1993).

The goal of teaching programming is problem-solving transfer, that is, users are expected to be able to apply what they have learned to solving problems that they have not been taught. Programming constitutes only a part of informatics. It includes a wide spectrum of human activities as well as teaching methods. For some researchers it is indistinguishable from problem solving and developing algorithms, while for others it means coding in computer language only.

Nevertheless teachers need to evaluate student programs. In the computer science educational community, checking program validity is usually based on testing a program on diverse test cases. Testing for batch-type problems involves creating a set of input data cases, running a program submitted by a student with those input cases, analyzing obtained outputs, etc.

There are two major approaches to the form of evaluating programming assignments: automatic and manual evaluation. The automatic evaluation is a method in which a computer program aids the teacher in grading a student's work and facilitates the feedback process. Manual evaluation is performed by human evaluators. It can be semi-automated where the teacher does (part of) the work, but the tool simplifies the process. The basic requirement for the automated evaluation is measurability of evaluation targets (Ala-Mutka, 2005).

In programming contests and olympiads testing is the only possible evaluation format. Due to a vast amount of submitted programs this is almost always done automatically. The typical approach for automated evaluation is black-box testing, which is based on comparisons of algorithm results to the correct one. A huge disadvantage of black-box testing is that an almost correct program with a small mistake may score zero points. However, the most important part of solving a task is the thought process, when the student discovers the idea of the solution.

It should be noted that the term automated evaluation is a much broader term if used outside the context of evaluating programming assignments. For example, automatically processing multiple choice questions is also an example of automated evaluation.

Automated evaluation of student-submitted programs

Currently there are a lot of students in different programming courses. Most of them are given assignments, which are based on creation of programs. Teachers are faced with a huge amount of student submissions, which must be analyzed and evaluated. There are solutions to this problem, which are rather complicated systems for automated evaluation of these submissions.

Use area	Requirements
Programming Courses	Course design and course management
	Learning environment
	Plagiarism detection
	Peer-assisted evaluation
	High-security sandbox
Programming Contests	Contest management; including advertising the contest
	Limited feedback during contest
	Precise run-time, memory measurement
	High-security sandbox
Programming Exams	Possibility to retest with slightly changed program
	Management of manually written points
	Real-time points analysis
	Work package administration for evaluators
	Minimizing differences between points written by different evaluators

Tab. 1. Main requirements for systems in different use areas

These systems were developed at universities for evaluating submissions to programming assignments given in the programming courses. Major reasons for automated evaluation were: a) the need for a higher quality of teaching (feedback in short period of time, objective evaluation); and b) the need to decrease amount of the additional work for the staff.

Current use of automated evaluation systems

Automated evaluation systems for student-submitted code can be used in rather wide areas of programming teaching.

Examples of such uses are: Programming Courses (including distance learning), Programming Contests (corporative like Google Code Jam or learning society organized like IOI – International Olympiad in Informatics or ACM-ICPC – International Collegiate Programming Contest), Programming Exams, etc. However, requirements for systems used in these areas are rather different (see Table 1).

Methods of evaluation in automated assessment systems

Generally most of the automated assessment systems for student submissions are based on black-box testing. This process is done by repetitive operations on a submission that includes compilation of source, and run with several datasets (and usually this is a comparison with the known correct answer).

Tests usually are prepared to demonstrate functionality in different conditions. Most datasets for tests can be assigned to the following groups:

• Simple datasets (program functionality easy to check by hand, easy to trace simple problems).

• Generated datasets (is algorithm suitable for different situations?).

• Atypical datasets (dataset is probably not expected by student, e.g., searching of maximum in set of the negative numbers).

• Large datasets (it measures efficiency of algorithm).

However, black-box testing has its problems. The most important was formulated by Dijkstra (1972): "program testing can be a very effective way to show the presence of bugs, but it is hopelessly inadequate for showing their absence." Black-box testing does not prove the correctness of a program, but the absence of *known* errors. Figure 1 presents other concerns.

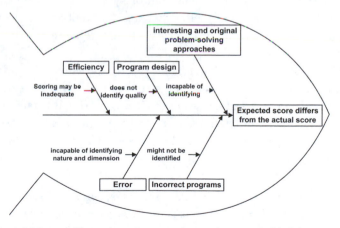

Fig. 1. Ishikawa fishbone chart: Concerns about and reasons for black-box testing

While at the moment there is no good alternative to black-box testing in automatic evaluation, nevertheless it is suitable to reach the main goal of testing: to distinguish correct and incorrect solutions and to distinguish different classes of correct solutions. Some concerns can be minimized by improving the quality of tests and score aggregation schemes. Also, it is a good idea to include other forms of evaluation and search for other options like providing more feedback to students and evaluators.

Testing functionality and efficiency

The most important aim of black-box testing in automated evaluation systems for student submissions is to check whether submissions are able to work and terminate, while at the same time providing correct output for every valid test given as an input. Such a feature is called *functionality*. Another important feature of submission is the ability to meet memory usage and time performance requirements in the worst case. This feature can be expressed in big O notation and is usually called *efficiency*. During the test development task authors take into account different possible solutions and associate them with some expected score. This usually helps them to create tests and assign them to one of the two groups (correctness tests and efficiency tests) with correct weights. Passing correctness tests means that the program is a functional one, while passing efficiency tests means that it reached the required efficiency.

Different scoring models of automated testing

Testing usually provides different measures of a student program. However, conversion of these measuring results to the final score can be a very different process. While the simple sum of passed test weights is rather typical as a final score, nevertheless there are different approaches. Some of them are more suitable for contests; others are more popular in the teaching environment.

Partial scoring is a scoring scheme for the black-box testing where points are assigned for each test run independently, and the score for a task is calculated as the sum of scores for each test run. It is typical to use different weights for different test runs and these weights are determined by the task creator in advance. Final score S is calculated according to the following formula: $S = \sum_{i \in T} w_i I_i$, here T – test run set, w_i – weight corre-

sponding to the test run i, I_i – indicates if the test run i is passed, $I_i \in \{0, 1\}$.

This scoring scheme was considered especially unsuitable for tasks, where a solution (or an answer) could be easily guessed. If the answer is easy guessable the student can print it without an algorithmic computation for all tests and try to score some points for an incorrect solution. However, it was the most popular scheme in olympiads in informatics and similar contests. Easy explanation of provided score and rather good distribution of scores are the major reasons for popularity.

All-or-nothing scoring is a Boolean scoring scheme that classifies the solutions into two categories: accepted (considered to be correct and efficient) or not accepted (incorrect or inefficient) without any intermediate values. Final score S is calculated according to the following formula: $S = \prod_{i \in T} I_i$, here T – test run set, I_i – indicates if the test run i is passed,

$I_i \in \{0, 1\}$. This type of evaluation is applied in ACM-ICPC-type contests and some teaching environments.

The problem of this scoring is that a very low percentage of submissions are passing all test runs from the first submission. The vast majority of IOI submissions are failing in at least one test (Kemkes, Vasiga, & Cormack, 2006). It shows that the use of such scoring schema requires the possibility of receiving feedback during the contest/exam. Otherwise it must be used in a complex mix with other measures like manual evaluation.

All-or-nothing batch scoring. Each test case consists of a set of test runs, and each test case is intended to assess a well-defined characteristic of a submitted program. This characteristic can be related to correctness and efficiency. If each test run has a binary (pass or fail) outcome, then a test case is passed if and only if all test runs are passed. Final score S is calculated by the following formula: $S = \sum_{j \in G} w_j \prod_{i \in Gj} I_i$, here G – test case set,

w_j – weight corresponding to the test case j, G_j – set of test runs in the test case j, I_i – indicates if the test run i is passed, $I_i \in \{0, 1\}$.

Other black-box scoring possibilities. There are also different approaches, which can be very useful for expanding possibilities of the black-box testing and providing more qualitative results. Some of them can be based on the previous three but with some specific augmentations.

Competitive learning approaches can be used in the black-box testing also. One of these approaches can rely on the idea: "the first gets everything, everybody who finished later will get less than predecessor." Such techniques can be applied in contests and in some learning environments like Moodle. This schema is more related to pedagogical aspects than technical ones.

The possibility of submitting *several submissions for the same task* can be very helpful for students. The feedback of several correctness tests can be presented to students. This can help to find some minor errors and only after positive feedback submission can it be handled as a candidate for all the rest test runs.

There are possibilities for using tasks that have several *parts with different answers*. A good example is a task that consists of several sequential subtasks, which increase in complexity. However, it is not clear if this is really helpful for students.

The score can be constructed in *relation to computer time required to solve specified test runs*. This can be very helpful if the student's solution is not far from the required efficiency, but is too slow to get all the points. Such a style of scoring can be helpful if run-time is fluctuating around required time.

Semi-automated evaluation

Some researchers found (Jackson, 2000) that the combination of two totally different approaches (automatic and manual) can give semi-automatic grading, which combines the talents of human and machine. As stated by Ahoniemi and Reinikainen (2006) semi-automatic grading can generate much better feedback.

We gained some experience in semi-automated evaluation systems for the maturity programming exam in Lithuania.

Evaluation of programming style

Evaluation of programming style is almost impossible without the use of semi-automated approaches. In order to automate this process some steps can be done if very strict requirements for programming style are formulated. Such requirements are not easy to reach as programming languages have several different popular styles for code justification, variable naming, and commenting.

In order to introduce the automated programming style evaluation, the elements of the style should be identified and concrete metrics for each element must be defined and associated with ranges of the expected values. A large part of style (including variable names and comments) can't be evaluated automatically.

Evaluation of algorithms

Some assignments require the use of specified algorithms, which are presented in course. There are approaches based on comparing block schemas of a known algorithm to a student-presented algorithm. However, evaluation can't be automated in full even in this specific case.

Programming exam in Lithuania

Lithuania's maturity programming exam is an interesting use case of semi-automatic evaluation. The research on exam data demonstrated that this approach is quite effective and still provides good quality of evaluation. However, this type of evaluation is still not very popular among computer science teachers and the outcome of this use case can be quite interesting for the community.

Informatics (named information technology since 2002) as a separate subject is taught in Lithuanian high (secondary) schools. The matura (school-leaving) exam in information technology (actually programming because reading and writing program codes is the essential part of the exam) has been carried out. The main goal of the national exam in programming is to encourage students to take an interest in programming and to develop algorithmic and structural thinking skills. When learning to program, novices are not only faced with solving problems, but at the same time also have to learn the syntax and semantics of a programming language, and how to express solutions in a form needed for computer.

Obviously, the contest system from olympiads can be useful, but it cannot be used without significant changes. The national examination centre has made a decision to create a totally new automated evaluation system with all the requirements met. Then another phase started – development of different modules responsible for the evaluation on different aspects, e.g., evaluation of the programming style. The development still continues, as the main rules of the exam change step-by-step and new ideas arise for better evaluation (see Table 2). One of the latest ideas is to integrate multiple choice and open question answer testing in the same system, by adding C++ language as a possibility for the programming part.

Parts of program evaluation	% of points
Testing. Automatic evaluation. *All or nothing scoring schema.*	0–80
Optional. Evaluated only if the results of at least one test are incorrect. Data structures, data reading, actions of calculation, printing of the results.	0–80
Obligatory requirements to the program (procedures and functions for single actions are indicated), programming technology, and style.	0–20

Tab. 2. Evaluation of the program development

Application of the evaluation operates with packages of solutions. Each solution must be processed as follows: It must be compiled, and then it must be run with several data sets. The answers provided for all of these data sets must be compared with the correct one.

Results of the exam are part of the competition grade when computer science or contiguous studies in higher education are chosen. Those who pass the exam successfully have wider possibilities for becoming students of computer science. On the other hand, it is a test whether a student is suitable for studying computer science: There are quite many first-year students who quit their studies since they find programming a hardly understandable and uninviting occupation for themselves. Discussion on the maturity exam in informatics has been presented at the ISSEP conference (Blonskis & Dagiene, 2006, 2008).

The exam may be approached in two ways: on the one hand, it is the evaluation of the results achieved by a student; on the other hand, it could heighten the motivation to learn. Both must be considered when planning the exam. The exam should be prepared so that it measures the competences needed for further studies in computer science. The exam is based on the optional module of the basics of programming, which consists of four parts: (1) introduction – basic elements of programming; (2) data structures; (3) developing algorithms; (4) testing and debugging programs.

The exam consists of two parts: The larger part (70%) is allocated to programming, while the remaining part (30%) concerns the issues of computer literacy. The programming part consists of a test (20%) and two practical tasks (50%). The aim of the programming test is to examine the level of students' knowledge and understanding of the tools required in programming (elements of the programming language, data types and structures, control structures, basic algorithms). Students should demonstrate understanding of existing code (Lister et al., 2004). According to many years of experience, the exam has a settled structure: 30% are allocated to knowledge and understanding skills, and the rest to problem solving. The problems are oriented toward the selection of data structures and application of basic algorithms to work with the developed data structures.

In the practical part students have to write programs for the given two tasks. The main aim is to examine the students' ability to master the stages of programming activities independently.

The first tasks are intended to examine the students' abilities to write programs of the difficulty described in educational standards. The abilities of students to use the procedures or functions as well as basic data types, to realize the algorithms for work with data structures as well as the abilities to manage with input and output in text files, are examined.

The second tasks are intended to examine the students' understanding and abilities to implement data structures. The core of the task is to develop the appropriate structures of records together with arrays. The abilities to input data from the text file to arrays containing the elements of record type, to perform operations by implementing the analyzed algorithms, and to present the results in a text file are examined. The operations are to be performed only with numerical values.

Code Evaluation

Tasks

Evaluation of the students' program codes developed during the maturity exam is the crucial point. The tasks of the exam are batch style – input is text file with a data set and output must be made to another text file (see Appendix). Students must write programs using FreePascal language (C++ was introduced in 2011).

The evaluation environment

Lithuania has good experience of evaluating students' program codes during the National Olympiad in Informatics which has about 400 participants. However, style of evaluation in a contest and in an exam is different. In contests participants are skilled programming students and even in this case there are some very low scores. It is clear that evaluation in an exam must be different from evaluation of non-functional programs.

The main difference between the concept of olympiad and the concept of exam is the idea of "fixing" small errors in a program. The problem with this "fixing" concept was that it is difficult to state if it is a small error or a big one, how many patches teachers can provide, etc. On the other hand, it is clear that after patching we must retest the program with all data sets, what is unusual for the olympiad and after this think how many points the student lost with this error.

A new automatic evaluation environment was developed in 2005. Development still continues, as the main rules of the exam change step by step and new ideas for better evaluation are arrived at. Two of the last ideas are to integrate multiple choice and open questions answers testing in the same system, and to add C++ language as a possibility for a programming part.

Automatic testing of code correctness

The evaluation environment is working with packages of solutions. Every solution must be compiled, and then run with several data sets. Answers provided for all these data sets must be compared with the correct ones.

The automated evaluation system performs evaluation in the following way: it compiles the program, prepares a safe environment for its execution, prepares input files, executes the program at the same time measuring its running time, interrupts execution if the program was running for too long, executes programs designed to check output correctness, stores all the execution and evaluation data for further analysis.

When preparing tasks for automated evaluation, the grading input data sets have to be prepared together with the accompanying program for evaluating correctness of the output to the grading tests.

In some tasks it is possible that several different outputs can be evaluated as correct. For example, the task is to find how to give an amount of money, if you have set of coins. In this task it is usually possible to find several solutions. In this case the evaluation program must check the sum of the selected coins. It is clear that checking the results of the solution program can be rather different from just comparison of two files. This gave the idea writing a separate checker for every task. As a result, evaluation application is not one but several programs. The correctness checker comes with a package of testing data and correct answers. It is possible to have some specific libraries, too.

Students usually make different simple errors in output format, e.g., forgotten spaces between numbers, all output in one line, etc. The decision was made to split the correctness checker into several programs: result format checker (which is a rather typical scanner as used in translators) and result evaluator. Both of them are prepared before examination by task authors. To ease creation of format checker a specific library is written.

The grading input data sets should satisfy the following requirements:
- Reasonably short and understandable to the evaluators.
- Identify incorrect solutions with high precision.
- Demonstrate the program functionality in various situations.

The program for evaluating output correctness should satisfy the following requirements:
- Be tolerant to minor inaccuracies.
- Identify the exact position of a problem or an error.

Alternative evaluation and semi-automatic testing

It is quite clear that automatic testing of students' codes is not enough for the maturity exam (Skupas & Dagiene, 2008). The problem is that most students are not at a high level in programming. Quite a lot of submitted codes are not functional even with the data set provided in the task description.

The evaluator team is trying to evaluate solutions positively. This means that students get points for their shown effort. For example: correct input output routines can be assessed with several points. Also, some points can be given for dividing the program to subroutines, for using complex data structures like array or record, for writing nice comments, for good programming style, etc. These criteria can be easily evaluated by a person, but computer evaluation is not so obvious. This is the reason for manual evaluation of solutions.

Several years' observation of the evaluation process of the exam showed that evaluators need an interactive semi-automatic evaluating environment, as some solutions only have some small syntax problems, like a semicolon missing (see appendix for an example).

During semi-automated evaluation, the evaluator can use the data obtained during static and dynamic analysis, modify the submitted program, and re-run the automated evaluation. At this stage the evaluator has to decide how significant were the mistakes of the candidates, which important parts of the assignment he/she solved, and which programming constructions the candidates mastered. At this point many problems arise due to splitting opinions of the evaluators, different level of their experience, etc.

It is highly important to prepare properly for this evaluation stage, i.e., thoroughly prepare and specify the evaluation scheme. However, it is not easy to prepare for the alternative evaluation, because the criteria have to:

- Be clear and unambiguously understandable to the evaluators.
- Exactly match possible acceptable solutions.
- Award the points to the candidates for the knowledge and skills they demonstrated.

The points for the criteria should:

- Correspond to the matrix of the examination.
- Be proportional to the weight of knowledge.

The use of small dichotomic (yes/no) criteria increases objectivity (Ahoniemi & Reinikainen, 2006). So usually criteria are corrected and divided into smaller ones after several packages of work of evaluators. Evaluated codes after this must be re-graded with modified criteria. The biggest problem of such an evaluation is that it requires a lot of human working hours.

Conclusions for teacher education

It is popular to use automated program-evaluating systems in the teaching of programming. A lot of papers on this topic were published in the last ten years. The survey by Ala-Mutka (2005) provides a comprehensive overview of these systems. *Journal on Educational Resources in Computing* (JERIC) published a volume with a lot of articles and a nice overview of automatic testing (Brusilovsky & Higgins, 2005). A group of researchers (Ihantola et al., 2010) updated the overview of Ala-Mutka. Most researchers agree that such tools can be very useful for teaching, arguing more on technological approaches and directions for further investigation.

We found that at the secondary education level such systems are still not very popular. So we decided to present some free examples, which are easy to use in a classroom.

Such systems can be divided in several groups like:

1) Everything prepared (including methodology and assignments).
2) Search for tasks and use them (tasks and tests are prepared for testing).
3) Use evaluation module for your LMS.
4) Create your own service (evaluation system can be installed to your server).

There are more systems than presented here, but these are the best samples for their group.

USACO's competition hosting environment (available at the website http://train.usaco.org/usacogate) has been developed by the USA Computing Olympiad. However, we can use it as a very comfortable tool for teaching algorithm basics. There are more than 100 tasks, which are put in good order. Tasks are grouped according to a theme and the student can't skip themes. Solutions must be submitted in C, C++, Java, or Pascal languages. The system is fully automated, but the teacher has no access to the student's work. The only possibility is to ask the student to show his/her account in the system (1st type system).

The users of UVA Online Judge (see http://uva.onlinejudge.org) can practice on more than 2000 existing problems and submit their solutions using C, C++, Java, or Pascal languages. It is also used for hosting online programming competitions. It is a good place for the teacher to search for task ideas; also students can test their submissions. However, the system still does not have a pedagogical role, as it is more like a set of problems without any guidance. The second problem is that it is not easy for teachers to keep an eye on students' work (2nd type system).

VPL – Virtual Programming Lab (see http://vpl.dis.ulpgc.es) is an example of another approach. It is based on the idea that the school or teacher has access to LMS Moodle. VPL is a module of Moodle and it also involves a virtualized grading machine, which must be run in the Virtual-Box environment. However, the whole system is more in the "do-it-yourself" style, as all tasks and tests must be prepared by the teacher. The big advantage of the system is the possibility of using standard interface for students and teachers; also the student login and learning data management is handled by the Moodle environment (3rd type system).

Mooshak (see http://code.google.com/p/mooshak) has its origins in ICPC programming contests. Also, it can be used in teaching. The results of the assessment can be publicly shown to other students. Grading is based on "all or nothing" and a partial scoring policy. However, it must be said that it is only a program and the teacher must prepare everything else (including server, task, tests, scoring scheme) (4th type system).

The most important observation is that most free systems still have some problems: some of them are good in test collections, others are good with integration, and still others are interesting in their flexibility. All these examples are in order of increasing requirements for teacher technical skills. It is worth mentioning that the preparation of algorithmic tasks, tests, and checkers for a student's program-provided answer is difficult and time consuming for young teachers. For this reason use of already prepared tasks for a young teacher in the classroom with centralized automated testing is highly recommended.

References

Ahoniemi, T., & Reinikainen, T. (2006). ALOHA – a grading tool for semi-automatic assessment of mass programming courses. In A. Berglund & M. Wiggberg (Eds.), *Proceedings of the 6th Baltic Sea conference on computing education research: Koli Calling 2006* (pp. 139–140). New York: ACM.

Ala-Mutka, K. M. (2005). A survey of automated assessment approaches for programming assignments. *Computer Science Education, 15*(2), 83–102.

Blonskis, J., & Dagiene, V. (2006). Evolution of informatics maturity exams and challenge for learning programming. In R. Mittermeir (Ed.), Informatics education – The bridge between using and understanding computers. *Lecture Notes in Computer Science,* Vol. 4226, pp. 220–229. Berlin, Heidelberg: Springer.

Blonskis, J., & Dagiene, V. (2008). Analysis of students' developed programs at the maturity exams in information technologies. In R. Mittermeir & M. Syslo (Eds.), Informatics education - Supporting computational thinking. *Lecture Notes in Computer Science,* Vol. 5090, pp. 204–215. Berlin, Heidelberg: Springer.

Brusilovsky, P., & Higgins, C. (2005). Preface to the special issue on automated assessment of programming assignments. *Journal on Educational Resources in Computing, 5*(3), Article No. 1.

Dagiene, V., & Grigas, G. (1993). Development of problem solving skills and creativity through distance teaching of programming. In G. Davies & B. Samways (Eds.), *Proceedings of the IFIP TC3 third teleteaching conference, TeleTeaching '93* (pp. 179–182). Amsterdam: North-Holland.

Dijkstra, E. W. (1972).The humble programmer. *Comunnications of the ACM, 15*(10), 859–866.

Ihantola, P., Ahoniemi, T., Karavirta, V., & Seppälä, O. (2010). Review of recent systems for automatic assessment of programming assignments. In C. Schulte & J. Suhonen (Eds.), *Proceedings of the 10th Koli Calling international conference on computing education research* (pp. 86–93). New York: ACM.

Jackson, D. (2000). A semi-automated approach to online assessment. *SIGCSE Bulletin, 32*(3), 164–167.

Kemkes, G., Vasiga, T., & Cormack, G. (2006). Objective scoring for computing competition tasks. In R. Mittermeir (Ed.), Informatics education – The bridge between using and understanding computers. *Lecture Notes in Computer Science*, Vol. 4226, pp. 230–241. Berlin, Heidelberg: Springer.

Lister, R., Adams, E. S., Fitzgerald, S., Fone, W., Hamer, J., Lindholm, M., McCartney, R., et al. (2004). A multi-national study of reading and tracing skills in novice programmers. *SIGCSE Bulletin, 36*(4), 119–150.

Mayer, R. E. (1991). Teaching for transfer of problem–solving skills to computer programming. In E. De Corte, M. C. Linn, H. Mandl, & L. Verschaffel (Eds.), *Computer-based learning environments and problem solving*, NATO ASI Series (pp. 193–206). Berlin, Heidelberg: Springer.

Skupas, B., & Dagiene, V. (2008). Is automatic evaluation useful for the maturity programming exam? In L. Malmi & A. Pears (Eds.), *Proceedings of the 8th Koli Calling international conference on computing education research* (pp. 117–118). New York: ACM.

Appendix – Programming task 1 in programming exam in Lithuania in 2010

Chess tournament *Maximum score – 25 points*

A chess tournament is organized at school. However, there are not enough chess sets. It turned out that some students have chess sets at home, but some white pieces are missing (none of the black pieces are missing). They brought to school the chess sets from home.

Write a program to calculate how many complete chess sets can be collected from the chess sets brought by the students.

A chess set of one colour consists of 8 pawns, 2 rooks, 2 knights, 2 bishops, 1 king, and 1 queen.

Input data

In the input file U1.txt there are several lines with integers.

In the first line there is written one integer – the number of students N ($1 < N < 100$).

In the following N lines there are written the numbers of the white pieces brought to school by the students. One line contains pieces brought by one student. The pieces are listed in the following order: pawns, rooks, knights, bishops, kings, and queens. Zero is written if the student didn't bring the corresponding sort of piece. In the example the first student brought 22 pawns, 3 rooks, 5 knights, 6 bishops, 2 kings, and no queens.

Output

Write the number of complete chess sets that could be collected from the pieces brought by the students.

Assessment of students' programs

Sample input file	Comment	Sample output file	Comment
4	Number of students	4	From the white pieces brought by the stu- dents, it is possible to collect four chess sets.
2 2 3 5 6 2 0	White pieces brought by the first student		
1 1 1 1 1 1	White pieces brought by the second student		
8 4 4 4 1 2	White pieces brought by the third student		
5 3 3 3 0 2	White pieces brought by the fourth student		

Directions

- It is *obligatory* to use one-dimensional integer arrays in the program.
- Write a function to calculate the number of chess sets collected from the white pieces brought by the students.
- Do not use statements for the work with the screen.

Program evaluation

First task: evaluation criteria	Points
Tests (Full points if the program provides correct outputs to all tests.)	20
Evaluated only if the program scores no points for the tests.	
Correct reading from file	4
The result is outputted correctly	2
The function, which calculates the number of chess sets that can be collected from the pieces brought by the students, is created	5
Other functions, procedures (if there are ones), and the main program are correct	9
Always evaluated	
The data type of one-dimensional array is declared correctly	1
The function that performs the indicated calculations is created	1
Meaningful names of the variables. Program parts are commented, spelling is correct	1
Programming style is consistent, no statements for working with the screen	2
Total	**25**

PART 3

IMPROVING TEACHING

7

THREE COMPUTING TRADITIONS IN SCHOOL COMPUTING EDUCATION

Matti Tedre and Mikko Apiola

Three traditions of computing

Computing as a discipline grew from three separate but intertwined traditions: the theoretical tradition, the engineering tradition, and the scientific tradition (Denning et al., 1989; Tedre, 2007). Over the course of time, various authors have tried to establish the importance of each tradition over the others. Firstly, the proponents of the theoretical tradition argue that the discipline of computing as we know it today would not exist without the work of Church, Gödel, Turing, or other pioneers of the theory of computation. Theoreticians emphasize the abstract ideas that form the foundations of the discipline.

Secondly, the proponents of the engineering tradition respond that without engineers the computing discipline would have no consequences outside academia, that without engineers computing would still be a compartment of mathematics, or that without engineers the stored-program paradigm would be just idle speculation. If one looks at the turning points in the history of computing, many of those turning points are due to technological breakthroughs, not only theoretical breakthroughs. Thirdly, the proponents of the scientific tradition argue that work in computing follows a cycle of scientific research similar to the scientific method: We explore and observe phenomena, form models and hypotheses, and empirically test those models and hypotheses.

The tripartite division of computing manifests in various forms. Educational programs have labels, such as computer engineering, computer science, computational science, and informatics. In software engineering there are debates between proponents of formal methods and empirical methods. Even the naming of the field reflects some traditions over the others: *Computer science* in the US stresses machinery, *informatics* reflects information processes, and the Dutch *informatica* refers to the junction of information and automatic processing. The same division can even be seen behind some debates on K–12 computing education.

This chapter concisely presents the three traditions in computing and analyzes their implications for computing education. Each tradition is presented with some of its underlying assumptions, application areas, restrictions, and weaknesses. This chapter aims at a balanced view of each tradition, emphasizes knowledge that computing educators should be aware of, and sticks to common computing terminology where possible. Epistemological and methodological understanding of the three traditions allows computing educators to align their pedagogical and practical choices to form a coherent whole.

The theoretical tradition

Modern computing was born in the 1930s and 1940s from a number of theoretical ideas presented by pioneers, such as Turing, Kleene, Post, Church, and Gödel. Mathematics is argued to be a quintessential skill for a computing professional (Davis, 1977; Ralston & Shaw, 1980; Hartmanis, 1993). Many of the pioneering ideas of computing are theoretical ones, and formal methods have proven invaluable for a large number of practical and theoretical purposes.

For decades after the birth of modern computing, there was a strong feeling that computing fields – including some of its practical branches, such as programming – are fully reducible to mathematics. For example, Hoare (1969) argued that computers are mathematical machines, computer programs are mathematical expressions, programming languages are mathematical theories, and programming is a mathematical activity. Similar views, where computing was considered to be a study of certain types of mathematical expressions, were also presented by other European computing authorities like Dijkstra (1972), Wirth (1971), and Naur (1966). Education was divided between academic education – which shunned practical topics, such as programming – and technology programs, vocational institutes, and junior colleges (Atchison et al., 1968).

However, criticism of the theory-centered view of computing grew steadily. In the 1970s and the 1980s those debates revolved around formal verification of computer systems. The formal verification debate was about whether formal verification can, in effect, be used to prove that a computer system will work correctly. The debates between a number of uncompromising formal verificationists and an eclectic bunch of their critics was brought to a head in the early 1980s by three arguments: that proofs in computing are products of social processes (De Millo, Lipton, & Perlis, 1979), that unlike theoretical constructions, the physical world is uncertain (Fetzer, 1988), and that there is a fundamental gap between models and the physical world (Smith, 1985).

The first argument reflected the work of Imre Lakatos (1976) on the philosophy of mathematics, and the next two are partially overlapping. The crux of those two arguments is that although one may be able to prove – in some cases and on the abstract level – correspondence between the inputs and outputs of a mathematical function as well as of a program text, executable programs do not evade the physical world: Computers are physical machines and programs are swarms of electrons. Most programs even have some kind of interaction with the world outside the computer.

Take, for instance, football-playing Lego robots, and consider correctness of a program in that context. Firstly, is the Lego program correct when the robot does exactly what it was instructed to do? That definition is not sufficient for correctness, because erroneous programs and bug-free programs both work exactly as they were "instructed" to work. Secondly, is the Lego program correct when the robot works exactly according to its model of playing football? That definition does not feel very good either, because in that case correctness has nothing to do with how well the robot plays football (the model can be broken).

Thirdly, is the Lego program correct if the robot frequently scores goals? That case is shaky as well, because it would make correctness a relative concept: Can we say that programs that score more goals are "more correct" than other programs? Fourthly, is the Lego program correct when its functioning fully corresponds with its specifications? In that case there is a problem with stating the specifications – should those specifications be of the kind "drive towards the goal and shoot a goal" or the kind "if the reading from sensor 1 exceeds 30, rotate motor 2 by 25"? Even if the program faithfully follows high- or low-level program specifications, nothing says that the specifications itself are correct.

In the debate around formal verification, by the end of the 1980s the formal verification movement was seriously running out of steam. Software engineering had been established already at the end of the 1960s, in the midst of the software crisis, and had, by the late 1980s, developed into a serious program of investigation and practice. Meanwhile, the scientific–modeling–experimental branches of computing were intertwining with other fields of science, creating new and exciting fields as they moved on;

102

take, for instance, biocomputing, cognitive science, and quantum computing. Gradually the formal verification movement abandoned its extreme position and moved towards the mainstream by acknowledging the limits of verification and by consolidating formal methods with the software engineering standards.

Although the formal verification debate was one of the defining features of the 1970s and 1980s disciplinary debates in computing, its implications should not be exaggerated. The formal verification debate never threatened the foundational status and importance of theoretical computer science. Questioning the importance of theoretical computer science was rarely if ever on the agenda; the issue was rather about acceptance of empirical and engineering methods in the discipline.

The engineering tradition

While theoreticians can claim that the birth of modern computing was due to the pioneers in the theory of computation, engineers too have an equally legitimate claim to the birth of modern computing: Many founders of Turing-complete, programmable, fully electronic computing machinery were electrical engineers. For example, John Atanasoff, John Presper Eckert, and Vannevar Bush all were electrical engineers. The roots of modern computing are in developments in technical topics, such as electrical instruments, automatic office machinery, nautical equipment, and measuring equipment. Among the turning points in the history of computing there are both technological breakthroughs as well as theoretical breakthroughs – take, for instance, the transistor, the microprocessor, and wireless networks.

The aims and central principles of engineering work differ from the aims of scientific and theoretical work. Engineers, whose job is to design working computer systems, have to take into account things that theoreticians do not, such as available material and human resources, and the laws of nature (Tedre & Sutinen, 2008). Engineering differs also from the natural sciences by its subject of study: Natural scientists typically deal with phenomena that have nothing to do with what people may think about them, while engineers deal with artifacts, which are created by people and for people. Engineering fields aim at producing useful things that fulfill some social needs or desires (Mitcham, 1994, pp. 146–147). Engineering also aims at contributing to processual knowledge about how to produce artifacts (Davis, 1998, pp. 7–8).

The map of computing disciplines today includes a number of engineering fields: computer engineering, software engineering, and electrical engineering (Ekstrom et al., 2005, p. 14). Whereas the value of electrical engineering and computer engineering has rarely been disputed, software engineering was, for a long time, considered to be intellectually inferior to other computing fields. One author called software engineering "the doomed discipline" (Dijkstra, 1989), another argued that it is based on anecdotal evidence and authority (Holloway, 1995), and third wrote that in their study, one third of software engineering articles failed to experimentally validate their results (Zelkowitz & Wallace, 1997). But over the course of time, software engineering became a legitimate branch of computing. However, the aims, premises, and methods of the engineering tradition of computing greatly differ from those of the theoretical tradition.

Methodologically speaking, engineers proceed by posing problems or goals, and by systematically following the design process to construct systems that meet those goals (Denning et al., 1989). The engineering cycle of work involves defining requirements and specifications, designing, implementing, and testing – or, in other words, analysis, synthesis, execution, and evaluation (see Figure 1) (Malpas, 2000). Parameter variation is one of the methods typical of engineering – in that method, the engineer alternates between measuring the performance of a device or process, and adjusting that device's parameters or conditions of operation (Vincenti, 1990, p. 139). Typically, engineers progressively and systematically narrow down alternative design decisions until a unique realization of the task is finally met (Wegner, 1976).

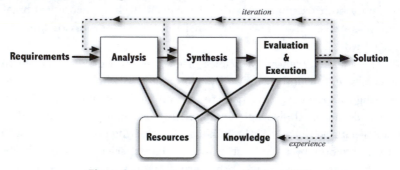

Fig. 1. Generic engineering process (Malpas, 2000)
Reprinted with the permission of the Royal Academy of Engineering, UK

The scientific tradition

Of all the debates concerning the soul of computing, the scientific nature of computing has been debated the most. Science has played a central role from the very beginning both by contributing to the development of modern computing but also by using computing machinery for scientific purposes. Science was also, from early on, in the focus of the disciplinary debates of computing. Already in the 1960s there were elaborate defenses of computing as a scientific discipline (Newell, Perlis, & Simon, 1967), the first departments of computer science were founded in the early 1960s, and in the 1970s the field was recognized as an independent discipline by the National Science Foundation of the US (Galler, 1974). Towards the end of the 1970s, the field was increasingly often characterized as an inseparable combination of theoretical, technological, and scientific aspects (Wegner, 1976). That characterization, perhaps most famously described by Denning et al. (1989), is still very popular today.

In the course of its development into a scientific discipline, there were numerous descriptions of computing as a science. Some argued that computing is an empirical or experimental science (McCracken, Denning, & Brandin, 1979), an "unnatural science" (Knuth, 2001, p. 167), an artificial science (Simon, 1981), or a natural science (Denning, 2007), and some claimed that computing forms a new domain of science altogether (Rosenbloom, 2004). Although among some circles there was a strong agreement that computing is indeed a science, there was no agreement on what *kind* of a science computing is. The reason is clear, too: There are numerous ways of looking at computing as well as numerous accounts of what science, strictly speaking, is (Tedre, 2011).

There is a broad array of arguments and debates about the salient features of science. The definitions vary between describing science as activity, as a type of knowledge, as an institution, as a style of thinking and acting, as a worldview, and as a profession. However, despite the amazing number of well-founded arguments about the nature of science, there is no commonly agreed definition of science. Yet, it is not an arbitrary term, either: Most scientists believe that scientific work should follow the *scientific method* – which is a collection of techniques, procedures, and methods for investigating the world. Most accounts of science also propose stages of scientific research: Those stages typically involve examining and observing things, formulating hypotheses or explanations, and testing those hypotheses or explanations. Figure 2 (on the next page) portrays the cycle of scientific research, where the empirical stages are on the left and the theoretical stages are on the right side of the picture.

In the debates between the three traditions of computing, there was significant opposition against the view of computing as a science. Some argued that people in computing fields are "just acting like scientists and not actually doing science" (McKee, 1995). Many said that computing is not a scientific discipline, but a synthetic, engineering discipline (Brooks,

1996). A lot of the debate, however, did not discuss the activities and aims of the discipline, but the name of the field. The naming debate spans from the 1950s at least to the 1990s (Weiss & Corley, 1958; McKee, 1995). Some opposed involving the term "computer" in the field's naming, while others opposed the term "science." The alternative names included, for instance, comptology, computics, informatics, and datalogy. Variants of some of those suggestions are still in use in various languages.

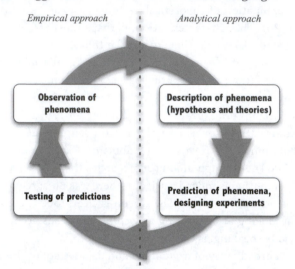

Fig. 2. The cycle of scientific research

The three traditions compared

In computing practice, the three traditions of computing overlap to a great extent. The engineering tradition relies on the foundations of the theoretical tradition, and provides tools for the scientific tradition. The theoretical tradition gets inspiration and open questions from the scientific tradition, and many of its developments are tested on computing machinery – as Donald Knuth (1991) put it, theory and practice live together and support each other. And the scientific tradition uses the frameworks of the theoretical tradition, and its experimental platforms are developed and provided by the engineering tradition.

Although the traditions are deeply intertwined, some differences can still be noted in the general notions underlying each tradition. Those differences are portrayed on the following pages and summarized in Tables 1–3. Table 1 presents the aims, concerns, goals, and outputs of each of the three traditions. Table 2 presents the *modi operandi*, methodological views, and operating principles of each tradition. Table 3 presents some of the fundamental assumptions of each tradition. As Tables 1–3 present somewhat stereotypical ideas concerning each tradition, one should note that each item in the tables can also be justifiably disputed, as most of the elements are neither unique to any one tradition nor always shared among all branches of computing within each tradition.

Goals and aims

Table 1 presents the aims, concerns, goals, and outputs of each of the three traditions. The theoretical tradition of computing works with subjects such as complexity, algorithms, and data structures. Its products are abstract ones – for instance, coherent theoretical structures and complexity proofs for algorithms. The main concerns are correctness of proof and coherence with the rest of the theoretical framework, and the tradition aims at extending theoretical knowledge in the form of, for instance, new, stricter limits for classes of computations and new algorithms for achieving tasks more efficiently.

Theoretical tradition	Engineering tradition	Scientific tradition
Aims at coherent structures	Aims at working implementations	Aims at new findings about the world
Concerned with coherence and correctness	Concerned with utility, reliability, and usability	Concerned with accuracy and validity
Extending and refining theoretical knowledge	Changing the world	Understanding the world
Algorithms and theoretical structures	Products and inventions	Discoveries

Tab. 1. Some goals and aims in the three traditions of computing

The engineering tradition works with subjects such as network systems, computer architecture, and software development. Its end products are tangible and they do various kinds of work – those products include things like microprocessors, computer software, and computer hardware. The main concerns are utility of products, their reliability, and their usability, and the field aims at changing the world by producing useful tools – improved products or new inventions – that fulfill a social need or desire (Mitcham, 1994, pp. 146–147). While the main aim is the production of artifacts, the engineering tradition has also epistemic aims and goals, especially knowledge about production and processes.

The scientific tradition works with subjects such as programs, models, and numerical methods. Its products are both abstract and theoretical – such as artificial intelligence implementations and computational models of phenomena. The main concerns are accuracy and validity between the models and the world, and the field aims at increased understanding of how the world works, as well as of how to model the world computationally. Discoveries in the scientific tradition include, for instance, cellular automata models of phenomena (e.g., Wolfram, 2002) and computational models for weather forecasting.

Concepts and principles

Table 2 presents the *modi operandi*, methodological views, and operating principles of each tradition of computing. The theoretical tradition proposes conjectures, and works with things like axioms and theorems by using analytical, deductive methods (the mathematical method of induction is also a form of deductive reasoning). The theoretical tradition is concerned with theoretical structures, and it works by using logical transformations between abstract ideas. Deductive reasoning cannot be done without having a solid foundation of proofs and axioms already established, and aside from open problems and conjectures, theoreticians prefer to publish results that are rigorously proven.

Theoretical tradition	Engineering tradition	Scientific tradition
Conjectures	Actions	Observations
Axioms and theorems	Processes, rules, and heuristics	Models, theories, and laws
Analytic; deductive	Empirical; constructive	Empirical; deductive and inductive
Concerned with structures	Concerned with processes	Concerned with causes
Transformations between abstract ideas	Concretizations of abstract ideas	Generalizations from particular findings
"Publish or perish"	"Demo or die"	"Publish or perish"
Rarely makes propositions that are not proven	Must be able to act under very little information	Reluctant to make claims if there is not enough information

Tab. 2. Some operational principles and concepts in the three traditions of computing

The engineering tradition takes actions, and uses processes, rules, and heuristics in those actions. The methods are empirical and constructive – many of them familiar from, for instance, design research. The engineering tradition is interested in developing, optimizing, and describing processes. The essential feature of engineering – the tangible products – are concretized from abstract ideas, although knowledge in engineering is also abstracted from particular instances. Instead of the academic proverb "publish or perish," the engineering motto has been articulated as "demo or die" (Hartmanis, 1993). Engineers are used to working with information that scientists would not consider adequate for scientific purposes (*cf.*

Vincenti, 1990).

The scientific tradition relies on observations, which typically arise from exploratory or experiment-based research. The scientific tradition works with things like models, theories, and laws, and is based on a cycle of empirical, inductive parts and theoretical, deductive parts. Science in general is interested in causes – in how the world works – and it describes those causes by generalizing theories and laws from particular findings. Scientists are notoriously reluctant to make claims without a wealth of evidence, and all scientific knowledge is considered to be tentative.

Fundamental assumptions

Table 3 presents some of the fundamental assumptions of each tradition of computing. The theoretical tradition is usually considered to be value-free in the sense that its findings do not depend on what people may think about those findings. In that sense, those findings are general and universally applicable. The nature of knowledge in the theoretical tradition is a tightly interwoven network of descriptive statements that are validated in their theoretical context.

Theoretical tradition	Engineering tradition	Scientific tradition
Mostly value-free	Often value-laden	Claimed to be value-free
General and universal	Partly generalizable	Highly generalizable
Reductionist	Holistic, can integrate competing ideas	Reductionist
Collection of validated inter-connected propositions	Propositional and procedural knowledge	Propositional knowledge
Descriptive	Descriptive, normative, and tacit	Descriptive

Tab. 3. Some fundamental assumptions in the three traditions of computing

As one of the aims of the engineering tradition is to create products that fulfill a social need or desire, those aspects are necessarily value-laden and about particular instances. There again, engineering knowledge about physical processes and material properties does not depend on people's opinions and is well generalizable. Whereas the theoretical and scientific traditions are reductionist by nature – complex things are explained by or deduced from simpler things – the engineering tradition is holistic and may even integrate conflicting ideas. Knowledge in the engineering tradition is propositional ("know–that") as well as procedural ("know–how") by nature. Researchers in the engineering tradition make both descriptive and normative statements; that is, they describe how things are, but also how things should be done.

Science is often claimed to be value-free, but especially in young research programs, researchers' views may significantly affect science (Feyerabend, 1975). As scientific research programs mature, they aim at increased generalization of their findings and integration with other disciplines. Knowledge in the scientific tradition is theoretical and propositional ("know–that") by nature, and its statements are descriptive.

Traditions in the teaching of computing

There are a myriad ways of teaching computing in the secondary school (Crawford, 2000). Some approaches are close to teaching of generic technology literacy (Dugger & Gilberti, 2007, pp. 166–174). Some guidelines promote application of ICT in subject areas (van Weert et al., 2000, p. 34). Some curricula emphasize programming, algorithmic thinking, and problem-solving skills (Tucker et al., 2003). Some educators prefer constructivist pedagogy, while others may prefer alternative pedagogical approaches. Some educators prefer knowledge construction using tangible instruments, such as educational robotics, while others prefer to start from abstract ideas, perhaps supported by on-screen tools and simulations.

There are various combinations of learning objectives, pedagogical approaches, educational resources, intermediate products, grading criteria, and types of educational technology for computing education in schools. Each computing curriculum for secondary schools promotes a specific view of those elements, and suggests a specific background education for computing teachers (Crawford, 2000). What is important is that the choice of educational elements should be well aligned within a tradition of computing, as mixing the traditions in teaching is not always straightforward. For example, the theoretical tradition is mostly concerned with propositional knowledge while the engineering tradition is more concerned with procedural knowledge. And if the intended learning objectives are of the procedural type, teaching and learning activities and assessment tasks should not be of the propositional type (Biggs & Tang, 2011).

For instance, if the learning objectives are about understanding construction processes and mechanisms of producing things, then also the rest of the curriculum must be well aligned with those objectives. The intermediate products can be, for example, Lego robots, programs, or multimedia shows, and evaluation of those products should focus on practical issues, including qualitative elements: utility, reliability, and usability (Table 1). In this case students would learn things that are related to the engineering tradition: the design process and heuristics, empirical and constructive methods, concretization from abstract ideas to tangible products, and the demonstration principle (Table 2). In addition to construction "know-how," students would also learn that their choices depend on preferences (they are not value-free) and that their work can integrate competing – even conflicting – ideas (Table 3). Although it is possible to integrate elements from all three traditions of computing, the epistemic and practical implications must be carefully weighed.

Example: K–12 computing education in Finland

Perhaps due to the short history of computing as a discipline, disciplinary understanding is rarely a part of teacher training. We present the case of Finland to exemplify this (see Jyväskylän Yliopisto, n.d., for further references). In Finland the teaching of computing subjects in schools began in the 1980s when personal computers started to become increasingly common. At first, the teaching of computing and information technology (IT) subjects was realized as computer clubs, and in the late 1980s IT was recognized as an elective subject in secondary schools. Every school had to provide elective courses for students on basic IT literacy, and some schools offered advanced courses, such as image processing and computer programming. In the 1990s the national curriculum saw a shift towards integration of IT education with other school subjects, while at the same time IT lost its status as a subject of its own. The national curriculum defined some general learning objectives on using the computer as a tool and on application of computers in subject areas. Schools were given the freedom to arrange teaching of computing as they wished. As a result many schools abandoned IT as an independent subject.

The current national curriculum of 2006 continues to stress the integration of IT education with other school subjects. The level of teaching varies greatly: On one hand, some schools teach advanced computing subjects, including programming, multimedia, databases, and even university-level courses in collaboration with local universities. On the other hand, there are schools where computing courses are not offered, but where computers are used only for finding information, writing reports, and showing presentations. Because the status of computing as a school subject is not clear and because coursework in computing courses does not contribute to students' future educational prospects, it has become difficult to set up permanent jobs for IT teachers in schools.

Concerning the reality of IT education, a 2008 study – done by an upper secondary school student – showed that 63% of schools offered courses in IT, and 48% of schools offered programming courses (Lappi,

2008), although a further survey found that many programming courses were realized at a very small scale. Although the Finnish association for science teachers (MAOL) has recommendations for IT courses in secondary schools, the main trend is integration of computers in other subjects (Kankaanranta & Puhakka, 2008). There are no pedagogical or practical guidelines to teaching computing subjects. In universities and research institutions there is little research on the pedagogy of IT or computing in Finland. The situation is very different in mathematics education, which has been the target of serious and sustained research effort.

The current situation provides a unique possibility for serious development of computing education in secondary schools, basing it on a sound understanding of the nature of computing as a discipline. IT teachers' professional development can be tailored to their skills, motivation, attitudes, and pedagogical preferences. One of the promising directions is to follow the engineering tradition and to align objectives, teaching and learning activities, assessment tasks, and grading criteria along that tradition.

Pedagogical approaches and teachers' professional development

Curriculum and pedagogical guidelines for computing subjects in K–12 education need to be founded on educational psychology as well as disciplinary self-understanding of computing. Disciplinary understanding can be developed by including, in teacher training, rich perspectives from each tradition of computing. Each tradition must also be accompanied with relevant pedagogical views from the pedagogy of mathematics, science, and engineering. Concerning new visions for learning, problem-based learning is a broadly used model for learning to cope with authentic, real-world problems (Hmelo-Silver, 2004); progressive inquiry utilizes scientists' modes of inquiry to learning (Hakkarainen, 2003); and project-based learning combines those two approaches together (Barron et al., 1998). Those approaches often use open-ended cases and projects, and they support divergent learning. Other well-aligned pedagogical theories include, for instance, constructionism (Papert & Harel, 1991), the self-determination theory (Niemiec & Ryan, 2009), and support for deep approaches to learning (Marton & Säljö, 1976).

Ideas from digital media, pair programming, computational thinking, visual arts, and computational biology can be used to stimulate teacher training for K–12 computing education. While project work and problem solving of the engineering nature – such as multimedia projects, robotics project, websites, programming, databases, creative writing, and demonstrations – are the most motivating for young learners, those pedagogical tools can easily be used to give students a richer perspective to computing, too. One of the well-tested engineering-based approaches – one that is rich in theory and modeling too – is educational robotics.

There is a significant international research base on using robotics in K–12 computing education. There are positive experiences on, for instance, Lego robotics, ranging from the primary to the tertiary level (Karp et al., 2010; Klassner & Anderson, 2003; Apiola, Lattu, & Pasanen, 2012). Using robots as a learning tool has been argued to support intrinsic motivation, creative problem solving, and self-regulated learning. The level of challenge can be adjusted to vary from very simple robot designs and programming tasks to university-level studies.

Although robotics as a learning vehicle relies on the engineering tradition, it can serve as a tool for the theoretical and scientific traditions, too. Examples of the scientific tradition include, for instance, experimenting with sensor information, weather observation, and other environment-related tasks. Programs can be designed to collect data, and to provide data for statistics, predictions, and generalizations. Examples of the theoretical tradition include, for instance, sorting problems, communication optimization problems, and other algorithmic tasks.

In teacher training and continuing education, a school or university department may hold a hidden ethos that elevates one of the traditions over the others. While such bias may have positive consequences on the department level, it is detrimental for teacher trainees. Intellectual traditions of computing are a root determinant of learning environments in computing fields, and that selection should be made in an explicit, transparent, and informed manner. Traditions of computing are also tightly connected with pedagogical approaches. One should seek for firm alignment of tradition choice, pedagogical choice, and learning environment design. When practicing their art, computing educators should be able to make informed decisions about their own teaching.

Acknowledgement. This research was funded by the Academy of Finland project #132572.

References

Apiola, M., Lattu, M., & Pasanen, T. A. (2012). Creativity-supporting learning environment—CSLE. *ACM Transactions on Computing Education, 12*(3), 11:1–11:25.

Atchison, W. F., Conte, S. D., Hamblen, J. W., Hull, T. E., Keenan, T. A., Kehl, W. B., McCluskey, E. J., Navarro, S. O., Rheinboldt, W. C., Schweppe, E. J., Viavant, W., & Young, D. M. (1968). Curriculum 68: Recommendations for academic programs in computer science: A report of the ACM curriculum committee on computer science. *Communications of the ACM, 11*(3), 151–197.

Barron, B. J. S., Schwartz, D. L., Vye, N. J., Moore, A., Petrosino, A., Zech, L., Bransford, J. D., Cognition, T., & Vanderbilt, T. G. (1998). Doing with understanding: Lessons from research on problem- and project-based learning. *The Journal of the Learning Sciences*, 7(3&4), 271–311.

Biggs, J., & Tang, C. (2011). *Teaching for quality learning at university: What the student does* (4th ed.). New York: Open University Press.

Brooks, F. P. (1996). The computer scientist as toolsmith II. *Communications of the ACM*, 39(3), 61–68.

Crawford, R. (2000). Information technology in secondary schools and its impact on training information technology teachers. *Journal of Information Technology for Teacher Education*, 9(2), 183–197.

Davis, M. (1998). *Thinking like an engineer—Studies in the ethics of a profession*. Oxford, UK: Oxford University Press.

Davis, R. L. (1977). Recommended mathematical topics for computer science majors. *SIGCSE Bulletin*, 9(3), 51–55.

De Millo, R. A., Lipton, R. J., & Perlis, A. J. (1979). Social processes and proofs of theorems and programs. *Communications of the ACM*, 22(5), 271–280.

Denning, P. J. (2007). Computing is a natural science. *Communications of the ACM*, 50(7), 13–18.

Denning, P. J., Comer, D. E., Gries, D., Mulder, M. C., Tucker, A., Turner, A. J., & Young, P. R. (1989). Computing as a discipline. *Communications of the ACM*, 32(1), 9–23.

Dijkstra, E. W. (1972). The humble programmer. *Communications of the ACM*, 15(10), 859–866.

Dijkstra, E. W. (1989). On the cruelty of really teaching computer science. *Communications of the ACM*, 32(12), 1398–1404.

Dugger, W. E., & Gilberti, A. F. (Eds.) (2007). *Standards for technological literacy: Content for the study of technology* (3rd ed.). Reston, VA: International Technology Education Association.

Ekstrom, J. J., Gorka, S., Kamali, R., Lawson, E., Lunt, B., Miller, J., & Reichgelt, H. (2005). *Computing curricula, information technology volume*. New York: ACM.

Fetzer, J. H. (1988). Program verification: The very idea. *Communications of the ACM*, 31(9), 1048–1063.

Feyerabend, P. K. (1975). *Against method*. London: Verso.

Galler, B. A. (1974). Letter from a past president: Distinction of computer science. *Communications of the ACM*, 17(6), 300.

Hakkarainen, K. (2003). Emergence of progressive-inquiry culture in computer-supported collaborative learning. *Learning Environments Research*, 6(2), 199– 220.

Hartmanis, J. (1993). Some observations about the nature of computer science. In R. K. Shyamasundar (Ed.), Foundations of software technology and theoretical computer science. *Lecture Notes in Computer Science*, Vol. 761, pp. 1–12. Berlin/Heidelberg: Springer.

Hmelo-Silver, C. E. (2004). Problem-based learning: What and how do students learn? *Educational Psychology Review*, 16(3), 235–266.

Hoare, C. A. R. (1969). An axiomatic basis for computer programming. *Communications of the ACM*, 12(10), 576–580.

Holloway, C. M. (1995). Software engineering and epistemology. *SIGSOFT Software Engineering Notes*, 20(2), 20–21.

Jyväskylän Yliopisto (n.d.). Tietotekniikan opetuksen historia. Retrieved December 10, 2012, from https://koppa.jyu.fi/avoimet/mit/tietotekniikan-opetuksen-perusteet/taustoista-nykyisyyteen/tietotekniikan-opetuksen-historia

Kankaanranta, M., & Puhakka, E. (2008). *Kohti Innovatiivista Tietotekniikan Opetuskäyttöä*. Jyväskylä, Finland: Finnish Institute for Educational Research, University of Jyväskylä.

Traditions in school computing education

Karp, T., Gale, R., Lowe, L. A., Medina, V., & Beutlich, E. (2010). Generation NXT: Building young engineers with LEGOS. *IEEE Transactions on Education, 53*(1), 80–87.

Klassner, F., & Anderson, S. D. (2003). LEGO MindStorms: Not just for K-12 anymore. *IEEE Robotics & Automation Magazine, 10*(2), 12–18.

Knuth, D. E. (1991). Theory and practice. *Theoretical Computer Science, 90*(1), 1–15.

Knuth, D. E. (2001). *Things a computer scientist rarely talks about.* Stanford, CA: CSLI Publications.

Lakatos, I. (1976). *Proofs and refutations: The logic of mathematical discovery.* Cambridge, UK: Cambridge University Press.

Lappi, L. (2008). Ohjelmoinnin opetus Suomen lukioissa. In *Academy of Finland national science competition for upper secondary schools* (Viksu) 6th best work in 2008. Valkeakoski, Finland: Valkeakosken Lukio.

McCracken, D. D., Denning, P. J., & Brandin, D. H. (1979). An ACM executive committee position on the crisis in experimental computer science. *Communications of the ACM, 22*(9), 503–504.

McKee, G. (1995). Computer science or simply "computics"? *Computer, 28*(12), 136.

Malpas, R. (2000). *The universe of engineering: A UK perspective* (technical report). London: The Royal Academy of Engineering.

Marton, F., & Säljö, R. (1976). On qualitative differences in learning – 2: Outcome as a function of the learner's conception of the task. *British Journal of Educational Psychology, 46*(2), 115–127.

Mitcham, C. (1994). *Thinking through technology: The path between engineering and philosophy.* Chicago: The University of Chicago Press.

Naur, P. (1966). The science of datalogy. *Communications of the ACM, 9*(7), 485.

Newell, A., Perlis, A. J., & Simon, H. A. (1967). Computer science. *Science, 157*(3795), 1373–1374.

Niemiec, C. P., & Ryan, R. M. (2009). Autonomy, competence, and relatedness in the classroom: Applying self-determination theory to educational practice. *Theory and Research in Education, 7*(2), 133–144.

Papert, S., & Harel, I. (1991). Situating constructionism. In S. Papert & I. Harel (Eds.), *Constructionism* (volume 36, pp. 1–11). Norwood, NJ: Ablex Publishing Corporation.

Ralston, A., & Shaw, M. (1980). Curriculum '78 – is computer science really that unmathematical? *Communications of the ACM, 23*(2), 67–70.

Rosenbloom, P. S. (2004). A new framework for computer science and engineering. *Computer, 37*(11), 23–28.

Simon, H. A. (1981). *The sciences of the artificial* (2nd ed.). Cambridge, MA: MIT Press.

Smith, B. C. (1985). *Limits of correctness in computers.* Technical Report CSLI-85-36. Stanford, CA: Center for the Study of Language and Information, Stanford University.

Tedre, M. (2007). Know your discipline: Teaching the philosophy of computer science. *Journal of Information Technology Education, 6*(1), 105–122.

Tedre, M. (2011). Computing as a science: A survey of competing viewpoints. *Minds & Machines, 21*(3), 361–387.

Tedre, M., & Sutinen, E. (2008). Three traditions of computing: What educators should know. *Computer Science Education, 18*(3), 153–170.

Tucker, A. B., Deek, F., Jones, J., McGowan, D., Stephenson, C., & Verno, A. (2003). *A Model Curriculum for K–12 Computer Science.* New York: ACM/Computer Science Teachers Association.

van Weert, T., Buettner, Y., Duchâteau, C., Fulford, C., Hogenbirk, P., Kendall, M., & Morel, R. (Eds.) (2000). *Information and communication technology in secondary education: A curriculum for schools* (2nd ed.). Paris: UNESCO.

Vincenti, W. G. (1990). *What engineers know and how they know it: Analytical studies from aeronautical history*. Baltimore/London: The Johns Hopkins University Press.

Wegner, P. (1976). Research paradigms in computer science. In R. T. Yeh & C. V. Ramamoorthy (Eds.), *ICSE '76: Proceedings of the 2nd international conference on software engineering* (pp. 322–330). Los Alamitos, CA: IEEE Computer Society Press.

Weiss, E. A., & Corley, H. P. T. (1958). Letters to the editor. *Communications of the ACM, 1*(4), 5.

Wirth, N. (1971). Program development by stepwise refinement. *Communications of the ACM, 14*(4), 221–227.

Wolfram, S. (2002). *A new kind of science*. Champaign, IL: Wolfram Media.

Zelkowitz, M. V., & Wallace, D. R. (1997). Experimental validation in software engineering. *Information and Software Technology, 39*(11), 735–743.

116

8

APPLYING STANDARDS TO COMPUTER SCIENCE EDUCATION

Carsten Schulte and Mara Saeli

Introduction

In computer science at school – sometimes also labeled as computing or informatics – goals, contents and methods are still somewhat unclear. In such a situation, the development, and definition of educational standards can help to build a community of teachers and support the community in improving computer science education.

In Germany effort has been directed toward the development of the so-called GI standards (*Gesellschaft für Informatik*, computing society), a proposal of standards for computer science education at secondary school. These standards have been developed as a joint work of GI members, with contributions from several local public workshops from all areas within Germany, and even from Austria and Switzerland. Both school teachers and university staff took part in this work.

Such a broad contribution of course affects the outcome. On the one hand the standards defined are in parts somewhat inconsistent, vague, or overlapping. On the other hand these standards are familiar to the community, because they were developed in a bottom-up process.

In this article, the effects of this bottom-up process are discussed, with a focus on implications for further developments in teaching computing and in teacher education. The framework of Pedagogical Content Knowledge (see Shulman, 1986) is used as a theoretical background. Pedagogical Content Knowledge (PCK) is the integrated teacher understanding of the subject (content), pedagogy, and features of the learners that affect learning this particular content. It is that expertise that allows teachers to represent the content of their discipline to their students in an effective way. Since its definition, scholars of different disciplines have positively accepted this construct and recognized its importance. Grossman (1989) reformulated the construct and included, in addition to the ability to reformulate the subject, other aspects that teachers should consider. These are the reasons to teach a certain topic, the content to teach, and the difficulties students encounter while learning such topics. In recent years, ICT and technology have been increasingly introduced in teaching. This means that teachers' knowledge of how to teach a certain topic (one of the aspects of PCK) requires further specialization in understanding how to use ICT to promote learning. This knowledge has been recognized as Technological Pedagogical Content Knowledge (TPCK, see Chapter 9 for further details). Though TPCK is a very important type of knowledge, necessary for those teachers willing to integrate ICT in their class, in this chapter we will refer to general PCK as it is the wider perspective and incorporates also instructional methods of teaching computer science without ICT, e.g., Unplugged (see Chapter 5).

The article is organized as follows: In the next section the GI standards will be presented, and the process of their development will be described. This will be followed by a short characterization of the result. The next sections discuss implications for teaching and the development of teaching material as well as for teacher education. Also, an insight on how the standards promote reflection on PCK is suggested.

Introduction to standards

Why are standards developed? The main reason is to define or set goals for education in a subject. Therefore such standards are often called achievement standards.

While this function – setting goals – is similar to a curriculum, standards define them in terms of competences, while curricula often define learning goals. In contrast to learning goals, which focus on knowledge, competences are the combination of knowledge, skills, and attitudes. In addition, competencies are understood to be valid with regard to a certain context or a range of similar situations. Competencies can be described in competence models, which define the aspects and levels of a competence. As yet, we do not have such competence models for computing education. Therefore we have a need for pragmatic competence modeling. The standards of the GI can be seen as an attempt to start such a pragmatic competence modeling.

The standards of the GI society

The standards for computer science education in secondary schools cover grades 5–10; students are 10 to 17 years old. The structure is inspired by the NCTM standards for mathematics education (NCTM, 2005), which distinguish between mathematical content and process, and also present a vision for good mathematical teaching.

Using this example, the standards for computing also present an outline for good computing education, and subsequently describe five content and five process standards, with several sub-items for each standard, plus an additional differentiation for grades 5–7, and 8–10. The items are described and further explained using examples like short outlines of teaching units, providing learning tasks or other directions.

Let us now take a look in detail. Table 1 gives an overview:

Content standards
1. Information and data: 1.1 Understand the connection between data and information and different forms of representations of data. 1.2 Understand operations on data, and interpret these with regard to the represented information. 1.3 Be able to use suitable operations on data
2. Algorithms: 2.1 Awareness of algorithms to solve problems in different areas. 2.2 Read and interpret given algorithm. 2.3 Design and implement algorithm by using fundamental programming concepts. 2.4 Represent algorithms
3. Languages and automata: 3.1 Use formal languages for interaction with ICT and problem solving. 3.2 Analyze and model automata
4. Computing systems: 4.1 Understand functionalities and structures of computing systems. 4.2 Be able to use computing systems properly. 4.3 Be able to explore new computing systems
5. Computing, man and society: 5.1 Perceive interrelations between computing systems and their social context. 5.2 Awareness of being able to make decisions in the use of computing systems; adherence to social norms in usage. 5.3 React to risks involved in using computing systems

Process standards
A. Model and implement: A.1: Create computer science (CS) models to given facts/issues. A.2: Implementing models with given tools. A.3: Assess models and their implementation
B. Reason and evaluate: B.1: Finding questions and hypotheses about CS issues. B.2: Give reasons for decisions on how to use computing systems. B.3: Use criteria to assess CS issues
C. Structure and interrelate: C.1: Structure issues by dividing and ordering. C.2: Perceive and make use of relations
D. Communicate and cooperate: D.1: Properly communicate CS issues. D.2: Cooperate in problem solving. D.3: Use suitable tools to communicate and cooperate
E. Represent and interpret: E.1: Interpret different representations of a fact. E.2: Illustrate CS issues. E.3: Choose suitable representations

Tab. 1. Description of content and process standards

In total, the standards comprise 188 competence goals. It is important, however, that the isolated competence goals are not meant to be taught one after the other. Instead they should be integrated to form a coherent approach to computing education. The idea and suggestion is to integrate a range of different goals into one teaching unit – e.g. by using certain processes to reach content goals. In order to support this, the standards are packed with texts describing this approach.

To give an example: With regard to information and data (especially "1.1 Understand the connection between data and information and different forms of representations of data") pupils should be able to understand and use principles for structuring documents and know basic object oriented concepts in class 5–7. In order to understand concepts in text processing, like "character", "paragraph" and "page" they can model such information using object-oriented concepts; and thereby they analyze which attributes are belong to which of the three classes. Note that this process is part of process standard A.1. The same idea of object-oriented modeling of a standard application is mentioned in the descriptions of content standards 1.2, 3.1, and 3.2.

Discussion of the standards

In this section, we discuss three aspects of the standards, which are implications of the chosen development process. These are: their overarching point of view, the competencies defined, and the role of the process in which the standards were developed. For these we will conclude there are positive as well as negative implications.

Implications from the development process

As already mentioned, many persons were actively involved in developing the standards. Based on two initial papers (Friedrich, 2003; Puhlmann, 2003) Puhlmann and Friedrich initiated the development of the standards. A group of persons made a continued effort to work on the standards, and regular meetings were held, supplemented by online collaboration, local meetings, and a beta test using an online feedback form. At the end, the standards were commented on and agreed by other groups within the GI, including the general board.

The overall size of the group of people participating is hard to estimate; the final document lists 89 "especially active contributors" plus seven "coordinators." Contributors were mostly teachers, while the group of coordinators was formed mainly by scholars. Coordinators were needed to edit the input and produce texts that summarized the ideas developed. In some cases smaller working groups tried to solve open issues and then presented (preliminary) results to a wider audience. At the end, the final draft was evaluated and commented on not only by the contributors, but also by other sections within the GI.

So overall, the development process used can be labeled as "crowd sourcing." This term from the modern web-world can be defined as "the act of a company or institution taking a function once performed by employees and outsourcing it to an undefined (and generally large) network of people in the form of an open call. This can take the form of peer-production (when the job is performed collaboratively), but is also often undertaken by sole individuals. The crucial prerequisite is the use of the open call format and the large network of potential laborers" (Howe, 2006). This procedure was used to develop and refine the standards of the German GI.

One major decision was to use the NCTM standards as a framework (see NCTM, 2005) to decide the discussion on several issues. After much debate, the structure with five process and five content standards was agreed upon, in order to move the development from discussing the general outline to a refinement within this framework.

In summary, quite early in the process the need for such a framework became obvious. Its purpose was twofold: to communicate a vision of the end result to the wider audience and to have a framework for sorting and structuring the manifold contributions.

It may not be obvious why the structure from mathematics was transferred to CS. It turned out that the division into five content areas was sufficient to discuss major topics, and that it provided a useful framework for structuring the standards.

Interestingly the following two structural issues were discussed most: programming, and the relationship between computer science and society. Both were not discussed in terms of adding a sixth area, but whether they should be implemented as content standards, or as process standard.

Overall, the development process used had implications (advantages and disadvantages) for the results produced, as listed in the following table. One effect of this process is, that it is easier to agree on things that are "nice to have", instead of agreeing on things that are not needed. Therefore the results describe a broad range of topics that can be included in the classroom. For a future refinement of the standards the task will be to shorten and compress the content.

Another effect of the development process is the presence of (small) inconsistencies. Due to the development process, the standards appear as

121

a bottom-up listing of isolated goals instead of a theory-driven top-down elaboration. However, teachers could feel the standards to be close to their school reality, as the voices of many practitioners were heard during the process.

-	+
Nice to have: Likeliness to include a goal instead of excluding it	*Acceptance:* Result is seen as internal process of the community, not as external threat, even when personal opinion differs
Inconsistencies: Bottom-up listing of isolated goals instead of a theory-driven top-down elaboration	*Alignment:* Overall, the result is in accordance with school reality, because many voices were heard during the process
Fuzziness: Terms are included, which allow different interpretations	*Idealization:* Incorporation of many practitioners' ideas: kind of "best of" of the current teaching practice

Tab. 2. Implications of the crowd sourcing

Implications for the defined competencies

The competencies defined (see Table 2) in the standards are meant as minimum standards. Every pupil should have the opportunity to achieve all (!) these standards during lower secondary school, at least on a basic level. The standards suggest that further elaboration by discussing more examples and issues in depth should also be possible.

The five content standards describe the discipline-specific competencies with a focus on content and concepts. The five process standards are describing discipline-specific practices and cognitive processes needed to engage in content. As the standards are prescribing competencies to be learned, the two lists should not be seen as lists of isolated aspects that could be taught sequentially. Instead the goal is an integration of content and process as an organic whole.

Within the current standards, content standards are in focus, and are described on a more refined level than process standards; the latter are rather vague and often not further explained with concrete examples. Content is still seen as somewhat superior to process, as content is more discipline specific and highlights visions of the nature of the discipline. In contrast, processes often quote general or interdisciplinary practices of thinking, working, and problem solving. They are, so to speak, less unique and therefore less important for outlining the core of the discipline.

So, while agreement on the general vision was easily achieved, drawing concrete conclusions for defining content and process was complicated.

However, as might have already been visible within the description of the general vision of the standards, a small but rather general decision was made to prefer the societal impact of computing over the practice of coding. And therefore implementation was not listed as content standard, but as a process – and, vice versa, societal issues connected to computing were not defined as a process, but as content.

This short presentation reveals two implications for the content or characteristics of the standards: (1) They are relatively abstract: it's easy to pretend their application without really adopting the intentions; and (2) There are some repetitions included, e.g., referencing Hubwieser's example of introductory teaching in computer science at school (Hubwieser, 2007, p. 113). This example is mentioned in at least three places throughout the standards. It shows that: (a) These are relatively vague definitions of the single standards; (b) The intention to demonstrate that teaching should NOT start to implement standard after standard in an isolated additive way, but that a coherent whole should be strived for; and (c) We do not have many examples suitable to be presented in the standards.

Note, the standards here have triggered a process to develop new teaching units, in order to implement the standards in everyday teaching practice. This is in sharp contrast to centralized standards, which are often neglected or ignored by teachers, and thus have to be tested, so that external testing is closely connected to the idea of standards. Here standards are having a motivational effect on the community of teachers to think about more suitable teaching units and to collaborate and to publish them (of course, also with the notion that such publications have to be reviewed and discussed by the community before they are published).

In summary, the effects (advantages and disadvantages) of this development process on the resulting competencies are listed below.

-	+
Examples: Not enough examples that are generally accepted	*Examples*: Missing examples triggered follow-up-activities, also within the community as a test of the standards
Abstractness: Abstracted coherent image of computing missing; triggered follow-up	*Outline of a coherent vision*: Integration of perspectives (CS vs. ICT; lower vs. higher secondary education, role of programming, of societal impact, and role of applications)
Goals direction: They are often not competencies but content-related learning goals without differentiation of levels	

Tab. 3. Implications for the characterization of competencies

123

Implications for the broadness and acceptance of
the educational vision developed in the standards

As mentioned in the introduction, standards can and should help to develop a shared vision about the key aspects of good teaching. With regard to this, Micheuz writes: "Without doubt, harmonization has a positive connotation, and is a worthwhile goal in many respects. This applies to the fragmented and seemingly chaotic organization of informatics education worldwide and often even within countries and schools, more than to traditional subjects." And in this context he refers also to the GI standards as a "major contribution for consolidating and structuring school informatics at the lower secondary level" (Micheuz, 2008; p. 325).

Due to the involvement of the whole community the vision of the GI standards is shared by the community and really used to think about changes on different levels of the educational system. Indeed, the GI standards are often referred to in panels or advisory boards discussing refinements of computing curricula in Germany on a local, state-wide, and even national level.

However, as a whole community has been involved in the process, it might be that instead of a shared vision only the lowest common denominator has been reached; and instead of a shared common vision only different, maybe even contradictory goals are listed without internal consistency – and in discussions one could easily point to some excerpt from the standards to back up the current personal point of view.

So the question is what (if any) is the shared vision of excellent computing education in lower secondary education that is expressed in the GI standards?

Answering this question is a kind of interpretation, based on the individual point of view on general education, which can be seen as criteria for evaluating subject-specific educational objectives. For example, in 1998 the mathematics educator Heymann presented a set of such abstract objectives for general education. These are: preparing for later life, promoting cultural competence, developing an understanding of the world, promoting critical thinking, developing a sense of responsibility, practicing communication and cooperation, and finally enhancing students' self-esteem (Heymann, 2003).

As in the NCTM standards, the first part of the GI standards elaborates on a vision of computing education. The first and most important goal is set as the ability to solve all computational problems that one might face in life. In order to realize this vision, the standards suggest that teaching informatics should adhere to criteria of excellence in teaching, as described, e.g., by H. Meyer in Germany (or by, e.g., Porter & Brophy, 1988, in an international context). The standards also point to the criteria mentioned in the NCTM standards, and discuss this in the context of teaching computing: equity, curriculum, teaching, learning, assessment, and technology (NCTM, 2005).

Of these general criteria, only curriculum should be briefly discussed. The section on curriculum suggests to take a look at the project Chemistry in Context (abbreviated as ChiK), which aims at developing teaching units for chemistry that integrate "Context orientation," "Cross linking knowledge to basic concepts," and "Methodological diversity" (ChiK). As in ChiK (some information is available at www.chik.die-sinis.de) the GI standards aim to balance two goals: (a) enabling students to cope with the widespread use of digital artifacts and information technology (IT) in everyday life, and (b) providing a foundation for learning computer science at more advanced levels (upper secondary; vocational training or diversity education). These aims of the standards can be implemented – as suggested – by "contextualizing" teaching and using "contextualized" curricula.

So the primary vision is to clarify and emphasize the role of computing in everyday life. Like chemistry, computer science is a "basic" science, describing and explaining the foundation of phenomena to be observed in everyday life. But unlike science, computing is also engineering, relying on teamwork to develop and implement computational solutions for virtually any possible domain. In order to demonstrate this aspect of the field, too, examples of "Computing systems" should go beyond the personal computer or the internet. And finally, computing is also an experimental science, designing simulations as a new kind of experimental research. The standards conclude that "understanding the world" (Heymann, 2003) requires understanding of this broadness of the computing discipline, too. (See Chapter 7 for a discussion of the different traditions of computer science. It is a good resource to estimate how ambitious teaching such an integrated perspective will be.)

In summary, the standards outline a shared vision of computing education, but on a rather abstract level. The concretization of this vision needs further clarification, e.g., by curricular development based on concepts (e.g., NCTM, 2005; Heymann, 2003; ChiK) mentioned in the standards.

Conclusion of the discussion

E-mail for you (only): Example of using the standards in teaching

The standards are a useful tool for thinking about goals of CS education and therefore raised enormous interest among CS teachers and educators at universities to develop teaching units or teaching models that embed CS education in everyday life, so-called context-based teaching.

The IniK (Informatics in Context) Project aims at developing teaching units that implement the GI standards. It's a loosely organized set of people at schools and universities; most of them were involved in the standard development. So in a way, this project is the second step of the standards approach.

Developing teaching units can help to implement the standards, as it supports teachers to change their teaching. In a way, this procedure is cheaper than constructing tests and conducting large-scale assessments of schools. And, secondly, teachers quite naturally are more intrigued by developing new teaching approaches than by developing material for evaluating the jobs of their colleagues.

In this section we briefly outline an example of such a teaching unit, as an example of using or implementing the standards in teaching practice.

The unit *E-mail for you (only?)* is targeting grades 8–10. In this unit students learn: (1) how e-mail is transferred from sender to receiver; (2) what risks are included in this technique; and (3) how to achieve privacy and authenticity in e-mail communication. The unit aims at two content standards (Computing systems (4); Computing, man, and society (5)) and one process standard (Reason and evaluate(B)).

In the first part of the teaching unit, learners are introduced to POP3 and SMTP, thereby gaining competencies to "understand functionalities and structures of computing systems" (4.1), to "illustrate CS issues" (E.2) and to "perceive and make use of relations" (C.2). The material suggests giving learners a list of messages of the mail protocol, like PASS <PASS-WORD>, which have to be ordered by the students, and then subsequently be tested using a prepared mail account via telnet. This example demonstrates two different outcomes of the project to define educational standards via "crowd sourcing":

Firstly, the result is really accepted "by the crowd" so that people are motivated and put effort into incorporating the proposed standards in everyday teaching. And as the crowd is largely built by teachers, the strategy to achieve this is not by external assessment, but by developing and testing teaching materials.

Secondly, the impact of the specific standard items is somewhat limited. There is a gap between the description of the teaching unit and the ascribed specific standards (e.g. 4.1, E.2, and C.2). The authors are first presenting 4,5 and B as the important standards that are to be achieved in this unit, but starting with the first part, other standards are mentioned as well (4.1, E.2, and C.2). This shows a somewhat fuzzy attribution of standards to teaching units. Or, to put it differently: The standards are not defined precisely enough to decide in a rigorous manner if a specific standard is likely to be achieved in a specific teaching unit. One aspect of this vagueness is that the standards as minimal standards do not list different levels of achievement, which would be a more precise definition.

The cell phone network: Example of using the standards in teacher education

For teacher education, the vagueness and inconsistencies of some specific items of the standards open a space to explore with prospective teachers.

In this example, student teachers develop a teaching unit about the cell phone network that aims to explore the standard information and data. Learners should be able to:

- "Understand the connection between data and information and different forms of representations of data" (1.1).
- "Understand operations on data, and interpret these with regard to the represented information" (1.2).
- "Be able to trigger suitable operations on data" (1.3).

The basic idea is to explore data emerging from the usual operation of the cell phone network and use visualization to interpret the data with regard to its information.

The unit has three parts: (1) uncovering the structure of the cell phone network (mobile station, base station, home location register), (2) visualization of location-based user data, and (3) discussion of privacy issues involved in location-based data and location-based services. The three parts are presented through examples. We report only part1: (Redaktion Schulprojekt Mobilfunk, 2008; p. 13), which presents a small experiment that can be used as a motivating introduction. Two cell phones and a metal box are needed. In a first experiment one phone is placed inside the box, which is closed. What happens if one tries to make a phone call to that phone? It wouldn't ring because it is not available – no connection from the other phone is possible. In the second version of this experiment, the second phone is – after dialing the number of the first – also put inside the box. What happens now? The same, because both phones cannot connect to the base station.

Overall these activities (producing different visualizations of the same data) should teach them a feeling for the information that can be revealed from data, and to introduce them to the first content standard, the difference (and interplay) of information and data.

Summary

Standards should raise the quality of teaching in a subject, by defining clear goals. Such definitions usually are based on a competence model describing the outcome, and tests for assessing the actual results of teaching. Therefore, typically, standards are constructed in a top-down fashion: Based on a predefined competence model, tests are constructed and employed. The case of the GI standards differs, as here the community of practitioners engaged in an ongoing effort to construct a competence model (see Tab. 1). Using such a process of crowd sourcing has two major impacts: Firstly, in contrast to a top-down process involving only few selected experts, the resulting model is likely to have some more inconsistencies, vagueness, and overlapping. Secondly, the result is not something external to the community and not connected to the (potentially threatening) prospect of external evaluation and external control over the goals and methods to be used in teaching. Instead the result is much more likely to be supported by the community. One effect here is the ongoing effort to develop, publish, and refine concrete teaching materials helping the community to put the standards in practice.

The standards have different roles in teaching and in teaching education. For the case of teaching, engagement in the development of the standards and teaching units helps teachers to focus on different aspects of the PCK of computer science:

While working in crowd sourcing, teachers have the possibility to think about the main topics/content to teach. Also, in the process to further differentiate the core standards, teachers are involved in both defining the content to teach in greater detail and also think about possible reasons to teach/learn certain topics. Furthermore, when teachers take part in the development of teaching units they are actively involved in thinking how to represent the content in a way that students can understand. Thereby they are also possibly taking into account students' difficulties and misconceptions around the topic.

Implications for teacher professional development

The role of standards for teacher education is manifold. Teacher education is not only about how to teach, but also about, e.g., understanding the goals of education. Standards are a useful tool to reflect on such goals, or broader, to reflect on and develop PCK. The GI standards provide student teachers with the opportunity to reflect on different aspects of PCK. By analyzing the standards, they are gaining insight into the content to teach and reasons for teaching it. Also, if they are then promoted to develop teaching units (or refine existent ones) they are engaged in reflecting on representations of the content and taking into account pupils' difficulties and misconceptions in learning such concepts.

Summarizing, standards can be a starting point in the process of student teachers' reflection on one's PCK.

In addition, standards demonstrate another role or task of teachers: innovation of current practice. Here the examples of the German standards are of special interest, as they were built by the help of in-service teachers, who made major contributions. In other words: They show how teachers are able to innovate, and provide awareness for the need for future refinements, especially in this dynamic field of study.

One possibility to trigger such reflection in pre-service teacher education is to let the students compare different standards, like, e.g., the UNESCO curriculum, or the CSTA standards.

For example, the CSTA describes standards from elementary to upper secondary education; level 2 (recommended for grades 6–9), named "Computer Science and Community") and level 3a (recommended for grades 9 or 10), named "Computer Science in the Modern World") are targeting a similar age range. The CSTA standards (Seehorn et al., 2011) distinguish "Computational Thinking (CT)," "Collaboration (CL)," "Computing Practice & Programming (CPP)," "Computers & Communications Devices (CD)," and "Community, Global, and Ethical Impacts (CI)."

Table 4 shows a comparison of standards, as an example of how students could do this. Such a comparison done by teacher students can help them to develop the following insights:

- One can see that computational thinking is very broadly defined. It has 15 sub-standards in L2, and 11 in level 3a. The three related GI sub-standards (Information and data, Algorithms, Languages and automata) together have nine sub-standards.
- The standards CD, CI, and CL have their counterparts in the GI standards. But CI follows a different conceptualization than "Computing, man, and society". While the GI sub-standards is more embedded in the discourse on socio-technical (IT) systems and their relevance for educa-

tion (see, e.g., Magenheim & Schulte, 2006), the CSTA seems to react more on the discourse on digital divide.

- Both standards respond to the question regarding the role of programming in school education. While CSTA introduces the sub-standard "Computing Practice & Programming (CPP)," the GI included "Model and implement" not as a content, but as a process standard. CSTA discusses modeling only as part of simulation, whereas the GI draws on the information-oriented approach (Breier & Hubwieser, 2002).

- Both standards respond to the problem of "ICT vs. CS," the misconception of computer science as the study of computer usage. In a way, both approaches try to add aspects of ICT to the subject computer science, but with the aim to prevent learners from confusing the two and to build a bridge from ICT to CS.

GI	Information and data	Algo-rithms	Languages and automata	Computing systems	Computing, man, and society
CSTA	CT			CD	CI
GI	Model and implement	Reason and evaluate	Structure and interrelate	Communi-cate and cooperate	Represent and interpret
CSTA	CT, CPP	/	CT (somewhat)	CL	CT (somewhat)

Tab. 4. Comparison of standards (dark and light gray areas indicate similarity)

Summarizing, for teacher education an analysis of standards and their implicit assumptions can be done by comparing standards from different backgrounds, and this provides an opportunity to build PCK. In-service teachers involved in the process of developing standards and/or teaching units implementing standards also have the possibility to reflect on and improve different PCK, namely: the content to teach, the reason to teach the content, methods to teach the content, and students' difficulties and misconceptions in learning the content.

References

Breier, N., & Hubwieser, P. (2002). An information-oriented approach to informatical education. *Informatics in Education*, *1*(1), 31–42.

Friedrich, S. (2003). Informatik und PISA – vom Wehe zum Wohl der Schulinformatik. In Hubwieser, P. (Eds.), *Tagungsband INFOS 2003 – Informatische Fachkonzepte im Unterrich* (pp. 133–144). Bonn: GI.

Grossman, P. L. (1989). A study in contrast: Sources of pedagogical content knowledge for secondary English. *Journal of Teacher Education*, *40*(5), 24–31.

Heymann, H. (2003). *Why teach mathematics? A focus on general education*. Dordrecht, Boston: Kluwer Academic Publishers.

Howe, J. (2006). *Crowdsourcing: A definition*. Retrieved December 10, 2012, from http://crowdsourcing.typepad.com/cs/2006/06/crowdsourcing_a.html

Hubwieser, P. (2007). *Didaktik der Informatik: Grundlagen, Konzepte, Beispiele* (3rd ed.). Berlin, Heidelberg, New York: Springer.

Magenheim, J. & Schulte, C. (2006). Social, ethical and technical issues in informatics – An integrated approach. *Education and Information Technologies, 11*(3–4), 319–339.

Micheuz, P. (2008). Harmonization of informatics education – Science fiction or prospective reality? In R. T. Mittermeir & M. M. Sysło (Eds.), Informatics education – Supporting computational thinking. *Lecture Notes in Computer Science*, Vol. 5090, pp. 317–326. Berlin: Springer.

NCTM. (2005). *Principles and standards for school mathematics* (4th ed.). Reston, VA: National Council of Teachers of Mathematics.

Porter, A. C., & Brophy, J. (1988). Synthesis of research on good teaching: Insights from the work of the Institute for Research on Teaching. *Educational Leadership, 45*(8), 74–85.

Puhlmann, H. (2003). Informatische Literalität nach dem PISA-Muster. In Hubwieser, P. (Ed.), *Tagungsband INFOS 2003 – Informatische Fachkonzepte im Unterricht* (pp. 145–154). Bonn: GI.

Redaktion Schulprojekt Mobilfunk. (2008). *Mobilfunk und Technik. Fächerübergreifende Sachinformationen für projektorientiertes Lernen. Klassen 5–10 sowie gymnasiale Oberstufe*. Berlin: Informationszentrum Mobilfunk e. V. Retrieved December 10, 2012, from http://izmf.de/download/archiv/IZMF_Projektheft_Technik08.pdf

Seehorn, D., Carey, S., Fuschetto, B., Lee, I., Moix, D., O'Grady-Cunniff, D., Owens, B., et al. (2011). *CSTA K–12 computer science standards revised 2011*. New York: CSTA ACM.

Shulman, L. S. (1986). Those who understand: Knowledge growth in teaching. *Educational Researcher, 15*(2), 4–14.

9

TEACHING SPREADSHEETS:
A TPCK PERSPECTIVE

Charoula Angeli

Introduction

Spreadsheets are computerized systems that have automated the record-keeping process. Learning about them in school is important, because they are an indispensable tool in the contemporary workplace. Traditionally, the teaching of spreadsheets, in K-12 settings, tertiary education, and teacher professional development programs, has had a technocentric and decontextualized focus, and aimed at mainly demonstrating the technical features of the computer application in relation to storing, calculating, and presenting information. As a result, students and teachers failed to recognize how spreadsheets could be used to support thinking and learning in various disciplines and content domains. What is the required knowledge for teaching spreadsheets in a contextualized way as tools that can facilitate the teaching and learning process?

In this chapter, Technological Pedagogical Content Knowledge (TPCK) is used as a framework that can help us understand the complexity of the required knowledge for teaching spreadsheets. The chapter reports empirical findings from a study that was undertaken to develop pre-service teachers' TPCK in the context of learning how to use Excel for the purpose of developing appropriate learning activities for learners ages 5 to 8.

Technological Pedagogical Content Knowledge

TPCK is an extension of Shulman's (1986, 1987) pedagogical content knowledge (PCK), and represents the body of knowledge that teachers need to have in order to teach adequately with technology. PCK, as introduced by Shulman (1986, 1987), identifies the distinctive bodies of knowledge for teaching, and constitutes a special amalgam of content, pedagogy, and learners. Central to Shulman's notion of PCK is how teachers' knowledge of learners, content, and pedagogy are blended into an understanding of how particular topics to be taught are transformed into forms comprehensible to learners and adapted to learners' characteristics, interests, and abilities. Thus, Shulman's conceptualization of PCK goes beyond the knowledge of subject matter *per se* to the dimension of how to teach subject matter taking into consideration learners' content-related difficulties. Transformation of subject matter occurs as the teacher interprets the subject matter, finds multiple ways to represent it, and adapts and tailors the instructional materials to students' prior knowledge and alternative conceptions.

Recently, researchers from different countries (Angeli & Valanides, 2005; Mishra & Koehler, 2006; Niess, 2005) argued that with the steady increase of computers in schools and the numerous implications of ICT in teaching and learning, the construct of PCK needed to be extended to account for the phenomenon of teachers learning how to teach with ICT. As teachers are required to learn new skills and techniques in order to transform their everyday teaching with ICT, ICT knowledge becomes another important category of the knowledge base of teaching, and any attempt to integrate ICT in the teaching-learning environment creates a need for developing PCK that is related to technology, that is TPCK.

TPCK, as shown in Figure 1 on p. 135, is conceptualized in terms of five knowledge bases, namely, content knowledge, pedagogical knowledge, knowledge of learners, knowledge of educational context, and ICT knowledge (Angeli & Valanides, 2005, 2009). Succinctly, content knowledge includes an understanding of the facts and structures of a content domain; pedagogical knowledge refers to broad principles and strategies of classroom management and organization that appear to generalize across different subject matter domains; knowledge of learners refers to their characteristics and preconceptions that they bring to a learning situation; knowledge of educational context ranges from the workings of the classroom to the governance of the school district; and ICT knowledge is defined as knowing how to operate a computer, knowing how to use a multitude of tools/software, and knowing how to use troubleshooting skills once a computer problem arises. While, as illustrated in Figure 1, there are a number of individual knowledge bases that contribute to the development of TPCK, TPCK is a unique body of knowledge that can be described as the ways knowledge about tools and their affordances, pedagogy, content, learners, and context are synthesized into an understanding of how particular topics can be taught with ICT, for specific learners in specific contexts, and in ways that signify the added value of ICT (Angeli & Valanides, 2005, 2009). Based on the results of empirical investigations, Valanides and Angeli (2008a, 2008b) suggested that TPCK is a distinct body of knowledge that goes beyond mere integration or accumulation of the constituent knowledge bases, toward transformation of these contributing knowledge bases into something new. Thus, the author herein supports the point of view that growth in the individual contributing knowledge bases, without specific instruction targeting exclusively the development of TPCK, does not result in any growth in TPCK (Angeli & Valanides, 2005; Angeli, 2005; Valanides & Angeli, 2006, 2008a, 2008b). In particular, TPCK, as a unique body of knowledge, is better understood in terms of competencies that teachers need to develop in order to be able to teach with technology adequately. These competencies are related to knowing how to:

1. Identify topics to be taught with ICT in ways that signify the added value of ICT tools, such as topics that students cannot easily comprehend, or teachers face difficulties teaching or presenting them effectively in class. These topics may include abstract concepts (i.e., cells, molecules) that need to be visualized, phenomena from the physical and social sciences that need to be animated (i.e., water cycle, immigration), complex systems (i.e., ecosystems, organizations) in which certain factors function systemically and need to be simulated or modeled, and topics that require multimodal transformations (i.e., textual, iconic, and auditory), such as, phonics and language learning.

2. Identify appropriate representations for transforming the content to be taught into forms that are pedagogically powerful and difficult to be supported by traditional means. They include interactive representations, dynamic transformation of data, dynamic processing of data, multiple simultaneous representations of data, and multimodal representations of data.

3. Identify teaching tactics, which are difficult or impossible to be implemented by other means, such as the application of ideas in contexts that are not experienced in real life, interactive learning, dynamic and context-situated feedback, authentic learning, and adaptive learning to meet the needs of any learner. For example, exploration and discovery in virtual worlds, virtual visits (i.e., virtual museums), testing of hypotheses and or application of ideas into contexts not possible to be experienced in real life, complex decision-making, long-distance communication and collaboration with experts, long-distance communication

and collaboration with peers, personalized learning, adaptive learning, and context-sensitive feedback.

4. Select tools to enable 2 and 3 above.

5. Integrate computer activities with appropriate learner-centered strategies in the classroom. This includes any strategy that puts the learner at the center of the learning process to express a point of view, observe, explore, inquire, and, in general, problem solve.

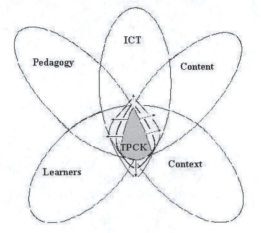

Fig. 1. A conceptualization of TPCK

Technology mapping as a methodology for developing TPCK

Technology Mapping (TM) is a methodology for developing teachers' TPCK. TM can be used to teach pre-service and in-service teachers how to teach with technology, and thus to develop their TPCK knowledge (Angeli & Valanides, 2009). In essence, TM, as shown in Figure 2 (overleaf), exemplifies learning by design and aims at enabling teachers to develop complex and interrelated ideas between technology and education (Blumenfeld et al., 1996; Brown, 1992; Dewey, 1934; Perkins, 1986; Zhao, 2003). TM engages learners in a process of developing technological solutions to pedagogical problems by allying teachers' pedagogical content knowledge with knowledge about the affordances and constraints of various computer-based technologies.

TM is a systematic methodology for designing technology-enhanced learning. TM is a dynamic, situated, and personal design process, because teachers' instructional design decisions are guided by a body of knowledge that is highly situated in the context of their real classroom experiences (Carter, 1990; Kagan & Tippins, 1992; Leinhardt, 1988; Moallem, 1998).

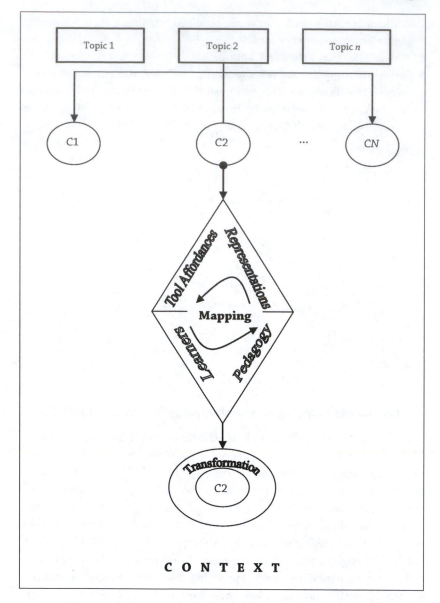

Fig. 2. Technology mapping (adopted from Angeli & Valanides, 2009)

As shown in Figure 2, context is an overarching factor in the process of designing learning with technology. Any attempt to design technology-enhanced learning is influenced by certain context-related factors, such as, teachers' beliefs about how students learn (epistemological beliefs), teachers' practical experiences about what can and what cannot work in a real classroom, teachers' views about the role of technology in teaching and learning, teachers' adopted instructional practices, school's vision, and educational goals. These context-related factors influence teachers' thinking about how the technology is integrated in the classroom. For example, if a teacher has deep-rooted beliefs in teacher-centered learning, then technology integration will most likely be teacher-directed (i.e., the teacher uses the technology to deliver information to students) and not learner-directed (i.e., the students use the technology as a cognitive tool to construct/represent meaning about something). It was deemed important to include *context* in the model, so that teachers can confront their potential biases and or constraints in order to be continuously reflective about the ways context-related factors may impact their designs of technology-enhanced learning. Furthermore, TM allows teachers to bring experiences from their classrooms into the design process, and, specifically, experiences that are related to teachers' PCK, that is, teachers' understandings of their students' alternative conceptions and learning difficulties in relation to certain curriculum topics, as well as teachers' understandings of their own difficulties in making a specific content teachable and easily learnable for their students.

In more detail, according to the model depicted in Figure 2, teachers are asked to think about a specific content domain, and, based on their experiences, to indicate their difficulties in making the most challenging aspects of the domain teachable to students, in connection with students' content-related difficulties. In the case of inexperienced pre-service teachers, teacher educators can provide them with a variety of examples from the literature on learners' alternative conceptions and the process of conceptual change. Subsequently, for each topic, teachers associate relevant content (represented as circles in Fig. 2) and tentative objectives based on learners' related alternative conceptions that need to be addressed. Then teachers are engaged in iterative decision making in order to think how to go about transforming the content with technology into representations that are more understandable to learners. In doing so, teachers need to first decide how tool affordances can be used to transform the content into powerful representations (upper part of the diamond), and how to tailor these representations for the specific needs of their students and use them by employing various pedagogical strategies in their respective classrooms (lower part of the diamond).

Mapping tool affordances onto content in order to represent it into forms that are pedagogically powerful is at the heart of the TM approach. Mapping refers to the process of establishing connections among the affordances of a tool, content, and pedagogy in relation to learners' content-related difficulties. Affordances are properties of the relationship between an agent and its physical environment – properties that allow and facilitate specific types of interaction. Gibson (1977, 1979) defined affordances as all action possibilities latent in the environment, objectively measurable and independent of the individual's ability to recognize them. For instance, a set of steps that rises four feet high does not afford the act of climbing, if the actor is an infant. Thus, according to Gibson's theory of affordances, affordances are action possibilities in the environment with respect to the action capabilities of an actor, and they are independent of the actor's experience, knowledge, culture, or ability to perceive. Norman's (1988, 1990) conceptualization of affordances diverges from Gibson's conceptualization in that Norman defines an affordance as something of both actual and perceived properties. The affordance of a ball is the round shape, physical material, and bouncability (its actual properties), and the perceived suggestion as to how the ball should be used (its perceived properties). When actual and perceived properties are combined, an affordance emerges as a relationship that holds between the object and the individual that is acting on the object (Norman, 1990). In accordance with Norman's conceptualization of the notion of affordance, TM maintains that in view of the fact that software affordances emerge as a relationship that holds between the software and the teacher who is going to use the software in his or her teaching, teacher educators need to make the connections among software affordances, content, and pedagogy explicit to teachers. The outcome of this complex instructional decision process will be a series of powerful pedagogical transformations, as depicted in the double-rounded circle in Figure 2.

Applying TM in the teaching of spreadsheets

Teachers who teach informatics constitute a special group of teachers, because they are technology experts by training, and technology is what they teach. However, their expertise, often times, is limited to the mere technical use of the tools themselves and does not entail the necessary pedagogical skills that will allow them to teach the tools in powerful pedagogical ways (ACM K–12 Task Force Curriculum Committee, 2003). The framework of TPCK can delineate the knowledge that teachers need to develop in order to teach spreadsheets in optimal ways and TM can facilitate their instructional design efforts. In particular, teachers need to (1) develop an educational rationale about why spreadsheets are important to teach, (2) understand the educational affordances of spreadsheets in teaching a particular content domain, (3) identify content domains that can benefit from the use of spreadsheets, (4) be knowledgeable of students' learning difficulties with spreadsheets, and (5) teach spreadsheets within the context of a meaningful curriculum topic. Succinctly, developing an educational rationale about teaching with a particular technology is important, because it sets the stage about how the technology will be used. For teachers who believe that spreadsheets are tools for performing complex calculations, the focus will be on entering numbers and formulas into the cells, whereas for teachers who view spreadsheets as tools to reason with, the focus will not be on the tool *per se*, but on engaging students in authentic meaningful tasks to reason with the tool (e.g., making decisions by comparing the outcomes of different scenarios). This, of course, has implications about the instructional design decisions that teachers will have to make about what content to teach and how to teach it. Moreover, teachers need to also be knowledgeable of students' difficulties with spreadsheets so they adapt their instructional plans and strategies accordingly. Research showed that students face difficulties with both the technical use of spreadsheets (i.e., with absolute cell referencing and functions) and with translating problems into appropriate representations during the phase of spreadsheet development (Hoag, 2008).

Context of study

In the study herein, a cohort of 24 pre-service teachers took an instructional technology course to learn how to use, among other tools, Excel in order to develop appropriate activities for learners ages 5 to 8. The challenge in teaching the course was twofold: Students needed to learn how to use Excel, and also needed to learn about the pedagogical uses of Excel in order to design developmentally appropriate activities for young learners. The research participants were in their junior or senior year of their undergraduate teacher education program and had thus the opportunity to take courses related to learning theory and methods in previous semesters.

Research procedures

TM was used for developing pre-service teachers' TPCK competencies. The course instructor first discussed in the classroom the philosophy behind teaching with technology. The departure from technologies as media for transferring facts and information to technologies as cognitive tools for constructing meaning and representing understanding was emphasized. Then, students were asked to think about topics that traditionally were regarded as difficult to understand or teach. Students were able to recall from their other teacher education courses and identified a number of suitable topics. Then, the course instructor introduced Excel as a tool with certain educational affordances for teaching and learning. Specifically, the course instructor discussed five distinct educational affordances of Excel, namely (a) Excel as a modeling tool, (b) Excel as a tool for giving feedback, (c) Excel as a tool for performing calculations, (d) Excel as a tool for organizing information, and (e) Excel as a tool for creating a hypertext story. Then, for each educational affordance the course instructor, with the help of the participants, identified curriculum topics and content for which there was research evidence that learners found difficult to understand or teachers found difficult to teach. For example, to illustrate the use of Excel as a modeling tool, the course instructor demonstrated how Excel could be used to model the phenomenon of the growth of plants, and the water cycle. Subsequently, the course instructor demonstrated each educational affordance with the application of a series of technical features within the context of a simple real curriculum example. Then, students were allowed to practice the same affordance with a new example of the same complexity as the one that was initially used by the course instructor. Subsequently, the course instructor demonstrated the same affordance with a new topic and content of increased complexity. Necessarily, a new set of more advanced technical skills was also demonstrated. This process continued with more examples of increased complexity until a new affordance was introduced. In essence, learning Excel and learning about learning with Excel was done concurrently within the context of a meaningful learning task. Succinctly, the instructional guidelines discussed above are shown in Table 1.

---

1. Discuss the educational affordances of Excel for the specific target group of students (i.e, Excel as a modeling tool, Excel as a tool for giving feedback, Excel as a tool for performing calculations, Excel as a tool for organizing information, and Excel as a tool for creating a hypertext story).
2. For each of the five educational affordances identify curriculum topics and content for which there is evidence that learners find difficult to understand or teachers find difficult to teach.
3. Demonstrate each educational affordance with the application of a series of technical features within the context of a simple real curriculum example.
4. Let students practice with Excel using a new example of the same complexity as in step 3.
5. Proceed with a new topic and content of increased complexity and demonstrate and or practice the same educational affordance with more advanced Excel features as needed.
6. Continue with a new educational affordance and repeat steps 2 to 5 until all educational affordances are discussed and illustrated.

Tab. 1. Guidelines for designing technology-enhanced learning with Excel

In order to assess participants' TPCK, students were asked to design and develop a lesson consisting of five learning activities with Excel, one for each of the five educational affordances.

Empirical findings

Students' design activities were evaluated in terms of the five educational affordances of Excel, namely (a) Excel as a modeling tool, (b) Excel as a tool for giving feedback, (c) Excel as a tool for performing calculations, (d) Excel as a tool for organizing information, and (e) Excel as a tool for creating a hypertext story. Ten points were assigned for each one of the five affordances. Thus, the maximum score for all five design activities was 50. Two independent raters assessed all five design activities and the computed inter-rater reliability was found to be .93, which was regarded as very satisfactory. Minor disagreements were easily resolved after discussion between the two raters.

Despite the fact that students never before designed learning activities with Excel, their performance on each one of the five educational affordances of Excel was high: (a) Excel as a tool for organizing information (*Mean*=9.83, *SD*=0.82), (b) Excel as a modeling tool (*Mean*=6.96, *SD*=4.0), (c) Excel as a tool for giving feedback (*Mean*=9.25, *SD*=2.54), (d) Excel as a tool for performing calculations (*Mean*=8.33, *SD*=2.41), and (e) Excel as a tool for creating a hypertext story (*Mean*=8.71, *SD*=1.59). As these descriptive statistics show, students' performance for using Excel as a tool for organizing information was the highest, and for utilizing Excel as a modeling tool the lowest. Paired-sample t-tests were performed and significant differences were found between students' performance on using (a) Excel as a tool for organizing information and as a modeling tool, $t=3.35$, $p=0.003$, (b) Excel as a tool for organizing information and as a tool for performing calculations, $t=3.30$, $p=0.003$, (c) Excel as a tool for organizing information and as a tool for creating a hypertext story, $t=3.12$, $p=0.005$, (d) Excel as a modeling tool and as a tool for giving feedback, $t=2.50$, $p=0.020$, (e) Excel as a modeling tool and as a tool for creating a hypertext story, $t=2.44$, $p=0.023$. Obviously, as the findings show, thinking about how to use Excel to model a phenomenon has inherently a higher degree of difficulty compared with using the tool as a means for organizing information, or providing feedback, or creating a hypertext story, implying that more time and effort should be devoted to teaching students about modeling and how Excel should be used as a modeling tool.

Students were asked to comment on their high design scores and all of them said that they found the approach of learning how to use Excel within a powerful pedagogical context very useful. Students S3, S5, S6, S7, S13, S14, S15, S19, S23, and S24 said that their experiences, prior to taking this course, with learning how to use a computer program was limited to learning how to use the tool in a decontextualized way with a focus on learning to use the technical functions of the tool. Students S1, S2, S4, S8, S9, S10, S21, and S22 said that an approach that is mainly focused on teaching the technical features of technology without making any connections to content is very limiting, because it does not demonstrate the educational affordances of the tool in teaching and learning a particular subject matter. As a result, students S11, S12, S16, S17, S18, and S20 stated that a teacher may know how to use a tool, but he or she may not know how to utilize a tool pedagogically in the classroom in ways that the distinct educational affordances of the tool and its added value are illustrated. All students pointed out that the educational affordances of a tool must always be made explicit by the teacher educator, because often times teachers' ignorance about the educational affordances may lead to the misuse of the tool in the classroom.

When students were asked to self-evaluate their TPCK, all of them stated that the course added to the development of their TPCK, because they now had a better understanding about how Excel can transform a particular content into powerful representations. Students S3, S5, S8, S9, S10, S15, S17, S20, and S21 said that this was more evident with utilizing Excel as a modeling tool, because they had to think about a topic that was difficult for young learners to understand and that was complex enough to be taught with models. Furthermore, when students were asked to reflect on their previous course experiences and trace the development of their TPCK, students S6, S9, S15, S19, S21, and S22 mentioned the educational technology course that they took during the first semester of their freshman year and said how difficult they found the course back then since they had no prior knowledge about the curriculum, learning theories, and in particular constructivism, as well as the instructional design process for developing lessons enhanced with computer tools. Nonetheless, students S11, S12, S13, and S14 said that their first educational technology course was pivotal in helping them do well in subsequent methods courses. A continuing struggle for them, students mentioned, is no longer how to find appropriate topics to be taught with technology, but to (a) understand in creative ways the educational affordances of a computer tool, and (b) map tool affordances onto content transformations. In asking the students to suggest ways of how their TPCK could be further developed, all students expressed the need to be explicitly taught about the educational

142

affordances of tools in the remaining of their teacher education courses, as well as to practice the educational affordances of the tools within the context of authentic design tasks.

Implications for teacher professional development

Teaching technology in contextualized ways is a complex task, because on the one hand instructors need to teach the tool, and on the other hand they need to teach how to design learning activities with the tool. TM can be an effective approach to be used in teacher education programs and or in-service teacher professional development courses, because it approaches technology teaching in contextualized and situated ways such that knowledge about tools, content, pedagogy, and learners are used concurrently in an iterative instructional design decision process. Based on the findings of the study, teachers must be trained in powerful learning environments where teaching is situated in real and authentic tasks directly related with the school curriculum, and in ways where teachers themselves are encouraged to reflect on their thinking, evaluate values and beliefs, and defend their designs as members of a larger learning and professional community. This way, teachers can be involved in exchanging perspectives, resolving dilemmas, and confronting uncertainty about how technology can transform existing classroom practices. The study also showed that teachers' TPCK is best developed when teacher educators explicitly teach the educational affordances of a tool, and when they explicitly demonstrate and model how an educational affordance can be technologically implemented. Also, in addition to using TM, asking teachers to design their own technology-enhanced learning tasks can also be an effective strategy to use as it forces teachers to think deeply about what content to teach with technology and for what reasons. Developing an educational rationale about what to teach with technology and how can be paramount to the development of teachers' TPCK. Additionally, teacher education methods courses must also capitalize on the importance of developing TPCK by making direct connections among the content to teach, how to teach it, and what technological tools to use to assist the teaching and learning process. Gradually, learners will learn how to transform content with technology into forms that will be more easily understood by learners. In other words, learners will gradually develop pedagogical reasoning about how technology can transform teaching and learning. Lastly, any teacher professional development program should provide teachers with a possibility of ongoing life-long professional development. This can be achieved by inviting teachers to participate in online communities of practice in order to share experiences, express concerns, and ask for advice whenever they feel the need to connect with other colleagues for assistance. Additionally, participating in online communities of practice enables teachers to see how other teachers use technology in their classrooms as well as to ask for advice regarding appropriate tools to use to meet specific instructional objectives. Undoubtedly, participation in online communities of practice makes teachers feel connected and not isolated. Consequently, feeling connected with others, who share the same concerns and strive for the same goals, positively affects the teacher's motivation and will to invest more time and effort in his or her technology integration efforts.

References

ACM K–12 Task Force Curriculum Committee (2003). *A model curriculum for K–12 computer science*. New York: Computer Science Teacher Association.

Angeli, C. (2005). Transforming a teacher education method course through technology: Effects on preservice teachers' technology competency. *Computers & Education*, *45*(4), 383–398.

Angeli, C., & Valanides, N. (2005). Preservice teachers as ICT designers: An instructional design model based on an expanded view of pedagogical content knowledge. *Journal of Computer-Assisted Learning*, *21*(4), 292–302.

Angeli, C., & Valanides, N. (2009). Epistemological and methodological issues for the conceptualization, development, and assessment of ICT-TPCK: Advances in technological pedagogical content knowledge (TPCK). *Computers & Education*, *52*(1), 154–168.

Blumenfeld, P. C., Marx, R. W., Soloway, E., & Krajcik, J. (1996). Learning with peers: From small group cooperation to collaborative communities. *Educational Researcher*, *25*(8), 37–40.

Brown, A. (1992). Design experiments: Theoretical and methodological challenges in creating complex interventions in classroom settings. *The Journal of the Learning Sciences*, *2*(2), 141–178.

Carter, K. (1990). Teachers' knowledge and learning to teach. In W. R. Houston, M. Haberman, & J. Sikula (Eds.), *Handbook of research on teacher education* (pp. 291–310). New York: Macmillan.

Dewey, J. (1934). *Art as experience*. New York: Perigree.

Gibson, J. J. (1977). The theory of affordances. In R. Shaw & J. Bransford (Eds.), *Perceiving, acting, and knowing: Toward an ecological psychology* (pp. 67–82). Hillsdale, NJ: Erlbaum.

Gibson, J. J. (1979). *The ecological approach to visual perception*. Boston: Houghton Mifflin.

Hoag, J. A. (2008). College student novice spreadsheet reasoning and errors. Dissertation, Oregon State University.

Kagan, D., & Tippins, D. (1992). The evolution of functional lessons among twelve elementary and secondary student teachers. *Elementary School Journal*, *92*(4), 477–489.

Leinhardt, G. (1988). Situated knowledge and expertise in teaching. In J. Calderhead (Ed.), *Teachers' professional learning* (pp. 146–168). London: Falmer.

Mishra, P., & Koehler, M. J. (2006). Technological pedagogical content knowledge: A new framework for teacher knowledge. *Teachers College Record*, *108*(6), 1017–1054.

Moallem, M. (1998). An expert teacher's thinking and teaching and instructional design models and principles: An ethnographic study. *Educational Technology Research and Development*, *46*(2) 37–64.

Niess, M. L. (2005). Preparing teachers to teach science and mathematics with technology: Developing a technology pedagogical content knowledge. *Teaching and Teacher Education*, *21*(5), 509–523.

Norman, D. A. (1988). *The psychology of everyday things*. New York: Basic Books.

Norman, D. A. (1990). *The design of everyday things*. New York: Doubleday.

Perkins, D. N. (1986). *Knowledge as design*. Hillsdale, NJ: Lawrence Erlbaum Associates.

Shulman, L. S. (1986). Those who understand: Knowledge growth in teaching. *Educational Researcher*, *15*(2), 4–14.

Shulman, L. S. (1987). Knowledge and teaching: Foundations of the new reform. *Harvard Educational Review*, 57, 1–22.

Valanides, N., & Angeli, C. (2006). Preparing preservice elementary teachers to teach science through computer models. *Contemporary Issues in Technology and Teacher Education*, *6*(1), 87–98.

Valanides, N., & Angeli, C. (2008a). Learning and teaching about scientific models with a computer modeling tool. *Computers in Human Behavior*, *24*(2), 220–233.

Valanides, N., & Angeli, C. (2008b). Professional development for computer-enhanced learning: A case study with science teachers. *Research in Science and Technological Education*, *26*(1), 3–12.

Zhao, Y. (Ed.). (2003). *What should teachers know about technology? Perspectives and practices*. Greenwich, CO: Information Age Publishing.

ABOUT THE CONTRIBUTORS

Charoula Angeli studied at Indiana University in Bloomington, Indiana, USA (BS in Computer Science, MS in Computer Science, PhD in Instructional Systems Technology). She is currently an Associate Professor of Instructional Technology in the Department of Education at the University of Cyprus in Cyprus. Her research interests focus on the use of computers as mindtools, technological pedagogical content knowledge, and the design of computer-enhanced learning environments. She has published extensively in well-respected referred journals and has participated in numerous research projects. In 2011 and 2012, she received the AERA/TACTL Outstanding Paper Award.

Peter K. Antonitsch studied at the University of Vienna, Austria (MSc in Mathematics and Physics Education, PhD in Mathematics Education) and at the Alpen-Adria University in Klagenfurt, Austria (MSc in Informatics Education). He is teaching Mathematics and Informatics at a higher technical school in Klagenfurt and is seconded to the research group of Informatics Didactics at the Alpen-Adria University in Klagenfurt. His research interest focuses on programming and databases, in particular on the influence of learning environments on learning processes concerned with these two classical topics of Informatics Education.

Mikko Apiola is a PhD student working in the field of computer science education at the University of Helsinki, Department of Computer Science. His interests include computer science education, improving programming education, and research on the different perspectives of computer science. In the past he has worked as a part-time teacher at the University of Helsinki, and as an Assistant Lecturer at Tumaini University, Tanzania.

Tim Bell, PhD in Computer Science (University of Canterbury, New Zealand), is a Professor in the Department of Computer Science and Software Engineering at the University of Canterbury. His main current research interest is computer science education; in the past he has also worked on computers and music, and data compression. He received the Science Communicator Award from the New Zealand Association of Scientists in 1999, an inaugural New Zealand Tertiary Teaching Excellence Award in 2002, and the University of Canterbury Teaching Medal in 2008. He is a Guest Professor of Huazhong University of Science and Technology in Wuhan, China.

Mordechai Ben-Ari is with the Department of Science Teaching of the Weizmann Institute of Science, where he heads the computer science education group. He holds a PhD degree in mathematics and computer science from the Tel Aviv University. He is the author of numerous textbooks, including *Principles of Concurrent and Distributed Computation* and *Mathematical Logic for Computer Science*. His group, in collaboration with the University of Eastern Finland, developed the Jeliot program animation system. In 2004, he received the ACM/SIGCSE Award for Outstanding Contributions to Computer Science Education.

Valentina Dagiene is Professor at Vilnius University, Lithuania (MS in Applied Mathematics, PhD in Computer Science, Dr. Habil in Education). Her research interests focus on computer science (informatics) education, and localization of software. She has published over 200 scientific papers and methodological works, and has written more than 50 textbooks in the field of informatics and information technology for schools. She works with various expert and work groups organizing the Olympiads contests. She is the Editor of the international journals *Informatics in Education* and *Olympiads in Informatics*.

Alexandra Gasparinatou, with master degrees in "Medical Physics," "Computational Mathematics and Computer Science," and "Education" received in 1995, 2003 and 2008, completed her PhD in computer science at the University of Athens in 2011. She teaches computer science in secondary education. Her current interests include the areas of computer science education and web-based adaptive learning environments. She has published in international journals, in international book chapters, and in proceedings of international conferences.

Maria Grigoriadou is now Emeritus Professor and head of the Education and Language Technology Group, Department of Informatics and Telecommunications, University of Athens. Her current research interests include the areas of web-based adaptive learning environments, ITS, and computer science education. She was the recipient of eight awards, has participated in 15 projects, and has four invited talks to her credit. She has a lot of international publications: 47 journal papers, 12 book chapters,

148

200 conference papers, with more than 1200 citations to her research. She is a member of IEEE, AACE, IADIS, EDEN, Kaleidoscope, and LeMoRe.

Djordje M. Kadijevich, with a PhD in Informatics (University of Novi Sad, Serbia) and a PhD in Mathematics Education (University of Joensuu, Finland), is scientific counselor at the Mathematical Institute of the Serbian Academy of Sciences and Arts. In 1992 and 1993 he spent one year at the Department of Computer Science (DIKU), University of Copenhagen, Denmark, studying the computer-assisted learning of mathematics. He is a member of the Editorial Board of the *Journal of Computer Assisted Learning* (2004–). His papers have appeared in international publications published by Elsevier, Springer, and Wiley-Blackwell, for example. For more details, please visit www.mi.sanu.ac.rs/~djkadij

Heidi Newton, BSc and Postgraduate Diploma in Science in Computer Science (University of Canterbury, New Zealand), is a postgraduate student in the School of Engineering and Computer Science at Victoria University of Wellington, New Zealand. Her research interests include computer science education and artificial intelligence. She has been active in supporting the introduction of computer science in the New Zealand curriculum.

Mara Saeli obtained a BS in Computer Science (University of Ferrara, an MS in Mathematics and Science Education (University of Amsterdam), and a PhD in Computer Science Education (Technological University of Eindhoven, Netherland). Her expertise focuses on the understanding of the PCK of computer science for secondary school. Her main interest is on how to use this knowledge to improve pre- and in-service courses and teaching material. Currently she is a research assistant at the Freie Universität Berlin, Germany, in the Department of Computer Science Education.

Carsten Schulte (PhD, University of Paderborn, Germany) is professor at the Freie Universität Berlin, Germany, and head of the computer science education research group. His main research interests include the conceptualization of computing education for the digital world; exploring computer biographies; and educational modeling of program comprehension. He has been involved in the development of standards for computer science education in Germany, and currently runs a project on improving pre-service computer science teacher education. In 2009 and 2010 he chaired Koli Calling, and is member of the editorial board of ACM's Transaction of Computing Education.

Bronius Skupas is a PhD student at Vilnius University in Lithuania (BS in Computer Science, MS in Computer Science) and also teacher of computer science at Vilnius Lyceum. His research interest focuses on the teaching of programming. He developed a semi-automated assessment system for student programs. He is a leader of the Lithuanian Olympiad in Informatics Technical Committee and a member of the Lithuanian Computer Society Council.

Matti Tedre works with flexible learning and the philosophy of computer science at Stockholm University, Department of Computer and Systems Sciences. His research interests include computer science education, research methods of computer science, social studies of computer science, the philosophy of computer science, and ICT4D (ICT for development). He is also a Professor of IT at Tumaini University, Tanzania, an Adjunct Professor of Computer Science at University of Eastern Finland, and an Adjunct Professor of Informatics and Design at Cape Peninsula University of Technology, South Africa.

SUBJECT INDEX

ACM Computer Science curriculum 67
algorithm *see* sorting algorithm
assessment 82, 85, 95

binary 69
Bloom's taxonomy 70

cell phone network 127
competence 118, 120–3; matrix 37–8,
    45–6; orientation 37–8, 45–6
computer science 5–6
Computer Science Unplugged 66
computing: concepts and principles 108;
    fundamental assumptions 109;
    Finnish education 111; goals and
    aims 107; traditions 100, 107–9
conceptual change 46–7
constructivism 66, 69
context: business 20–2; educational 25–8
crowdsourcing 121, 126

data quality 22–3
database examples 39–40, 42–4
design 136–7, 139–41, 143; instructional
    136, 139, 143

education *see* general education
e-mail 126–7
engineering 103; process 104
error correcting code 66
errors *see* spreadsheet errors
evaluation: automated 84;
    program-evaluating system 94;
    semi-automated 88, 93
experimentation: active 12–13

formal verification debate 101–3

general education 125–6
good tasks 42–3

implications: educational 14–15;
    pedagogical 61–4; teacher education
    30–1, 94–5; teacher professional
    development 47–8, 128–30
instructional patterns 35–6, 39, 47

kinesthetic 67

learning: environment 7–10, 38–42, 44,
    47; measurement of 4; pattern 38–40,
    42–7; personalization 35, 38, 45–8
levels of understanding 3

method *see* scientific method
methodical considerations 40–2
methodology 135–6
minimalism 31
model: construction-integration 3–6;
    mental 62; scoring 86; situation 3–4;
    text base 3–4
modeling: database 39–40; object-oriented
    120; spreadsheet 25–9; tool 140–2

New Zealand computer science standards
    76

parity 66
pattern *see* instructional patterns
Pedagogical Content Knowledge 117–18,
    129–30, 132–3, 137
pedagogy 113
phenomenography 61
problem: solving 82, 83, 90; structuring
    28–30